The Kenneth Williams Scrapbook

Adam Endacott

First published in 2021 by Fantom Publishing an imprint of Fantom Films Ltd
fantompublishing.co.uk

© Adam Endacott 2021

Adam Endacott has asserted his moral right to be identified as the author of this work in accordance with the Copyright, Designs and Patents Act 1988.

All rights reserved.

Every effort has been made to trace the present copyright holders of the photographs and illustrative material herein. We apologise in advance for any unintentional omission and will be pleased to insert the appropriate acknowledgment to companies or individuals in any subsequent edition of this publication.

A catalogue record for this book is available from the British Library.

ISBN 978-1-78196-378-4

Design, layout and typeset by Darkhorse Design, Liverpool

Printed and bound by Instant Print

Contents

Foreword by Christopher Biggins	v
Foreword by Sir Tim Rice	vi
Foreword by Morris Bright MBE	viii
Introduction	xi
Kenneth's Family Tree	xii

Kenneth's Scrapbook

Kenneth, My Godfather by Robert Chidell	115
Kenneth, My friend by Barbara Waslin-Ashbridge	116
Meeting Kenneth by Nick Lewis	119
Afterword by Robin Sebastian	120
Afterword by Bill Holland	122
Acknowledgements	124
List of Illustrations	125

This book is dedicated to Michael Whittaker, who Kenneth wisely described as the 'best of people', for his unfailing support, encouragement and friendship – thank you for believing in me all those years ago.

To my friend, Craig McWilliam, who joined me for a Guinness in The Boot pub one evening and we came up with the idea for this volume – "cheers me dear"!

To the memory of Michael Anderson who was simply lovely; so very kind and great company and Dame Barbara Windsor MBE for her support and being our very own Cockney sparrow – both reunited with their good chum Kenneth.

Michael W Anderson
1929-2019

Foreword by Christopher Biggins

What Adam Endacott has done in writing *The Kenneth Williams Scrapbook* is, I think, absolutely wonderful – it really gets the essence of what Kenneth Williams was all about.

He was funny, in fact, extremely funny.

He was bright.

He was unique.

He was adorable.

He was a good friend.

He was everybody's idea of a good laugh! In the Scrapbook you get every moment of Kenneth and the essence of him in so many ways, punched every time from each area – it sums him up perfectly.

I was lucky to know him as a friend and often had lunch with him and his mother, Lou, at Joe Allen Restaurant, which was a real joy. He could be a little off the edge at times, but that was him and we adored him for it. In a way, he actually was a scrapbook and this has captured him so brilliantly – so many memories and anecdotes.

I fully recommend this book, even if you don't like Kenneth Williams! It is expertly curated and a wonderful work to accompany *The Kenneth Williams Companion*.

I hope you enjoy it as much as I did.

Christopher Biggins
London, 2021

Foreword by Sir Tim Rice

It is a great honour to be invited to write a foreword to Adam Endacott's *The Kenneth Williams Scrapbook*. Almost inevitably, bearing in mind I am English and a generation younger than Kenneth, I was (and remain) a huge admirer of this complex and brilliant man. Only this morning, in summer 2021, that wonderful radio sketch from the 1950s, in which Kenneth finds himself clinging onto the fuselage of a plane with Tony Hancock in the unlikely role of test pilot, reappeared on Radio Four.

As is the case with *Hancock's Half Hour*, whenever I listen to a recording of Kenneth Horne's timeless *Round The Horne*, the superb star performances of the man in the show's title is very often upstaged by the Williams characters, allegedly the supporting cast.

It is no criticism of the masterful performances of Tony Hancock and Kenneth Horne, to say that in the intervening decades their stars have gently faded, whereas that of Kenneth Williams is still bright. This is not just because of his leading roles in so many of the Carry On films from 1958 to 1978, but because Kenneth the person, rather than just Kenneth the actor, made such an impact during, and after, those manic years of filming on a shoestring.

Thanks to many radio and television appearances as himself, most memorably on BBC Radio 4's *Just A Minute*, but also on numerous talk shows from *Parkinson* downwards, listeners and viewers, admirers old and new, came to realise that here was an intellectual and fascinating man who darted from double-entendre to sophisticated and informed social and historical observation, with the insight of an psychologist and the verbal skills of an unusually well-informed academic. Wit and wisdom were rarely so delightfully mingled, and occasionally mangled too.

I first met Kenneth as a nervous débutant on *Just A Minute* (me, not Kenneth) and although his formidable ability to dominate the show, through a dazzling command of language and pre-Wikipedia breadth of knowledge, was enough to make a newcomer apprehensive, his team spirit kept surfacing unexpectedly which enabled this beginner to settle in. I quickly discovered that if he was rude to you on or off stage it meant you were worth being rude to. Nonetheless, I thought perhaps I had irrevocably offended the show's superstar during one of my early appearances, when just before going on stage to record the programme, Kenneth remarked that we had an all-male cast that night. "Well, almost" was my too-speedy response which I immediately felt was a faux pas too far. But Kenneth, having feigned shock, repeated my comment to the audience five minutes later who loved it and I think made him begin to revise his diarised opinion after my first appearance that I was a "non-starter".

The occasional comments about me in his masterful diaries improved over the years. He recalled that I had cheered him with a letter from America. In 1988, when I was in New York for a few weeks working on the Broadway version of my musical written with ABBA's Bjorn Ulvaeus and Benny Andersson, *Chess*, it was clear to me fairly early in the rehearsal period that the show was not going to set New York alight, at least not with praise. When barricaded in my lonely hotel room to write yet more last-minute lyrics for yet another scene, I knew would not work, I read Kenneth's book *Acid Drops* and wrote him a letter telling him that it was the only enjoyable aspect of my current situation. On return to England, a beautifully hand-written reply was waiting for me (obviously this was in the late lamented pre-email era). It is to my eternal regret that I managed to lose his generous letter for Kenneth died just a few days later, four days after the show's first preview on Broadway. It must have been one of the last he ever wrote.

The man who made millions laugh portraying characters as disparate as Julius Caesar in *Carry On Cleo* and harassed travel agent Stuart Farquhar in *Carry On Abroad*, (although he managed to make them both insanely believable while playing them identically), was beyond doubt one of the great entertainers of my lifetime and I was very fortunate to have known him, albeit on his perfectly reasonable terms. His private life was that and more – I could not begun to have claimed that he was a friend but my thoughts of him could not be more friendly and no-one who knew him could have resented the way he kept his distance so originally and so amusingly.

Adam Endacott has done the great man proud.

Sir Tim Rice
Cornwall, 2021

Foreword by Morris Bright MBE

It was my first secondary school English lesson. For the teacher to get to know his new cohort, our ability and legibility, we were all asked to hand write an imaginary letter to someone that we would like to be a guest at the annual Speech Day. Most of my classmates chose a footballer or pop star. My imaginary letter was to Kenneth Williams. It was 1977 and I was eleven.

Eight years on, it is the end of August 1985 and I am in a year off before going to drama school. I had been to WH Smith to buy my first hardback book. Hardback books were expensive especially for a 19 year old saving up for his further education. The book was Kenneth Williams' autobiography, *Just Williams*. I purchased it on the very day it hit the shops. I had a ticket to see *Just A Minute* that week. I took the book with me on the off chance I got an opportunity to meet my comedy hero.

The show was not being recorded in its then usual location, the BBC Paris Studios, in the West End due to a major refurbishment. Instead, the recording took place at the Westminster Theatre a short distance away. I managed to get a reasonable seat but with the cast on a raised stage and in a larger theatre setting I feared any hope at getting close to Kenneth was all but over.

Then I saw that one of the other guests on the show was Barry Cryer. After leaving school, one of the jobs I had in my year off was as a barrister's clerk taking notes in court. I was in Southwark Crown Court one day when suddenly a host of well-known faces started to walk past me including Hugh Manning who played the vicar in Emmerdale (when it still had the word Farm in the title) actor Alfred Marks and comedian Barry Cryer. They were giving evidence for the prosecution in a fraud case. I ended up helping Barry and the others fill out their daily expense chitties.

At the end of the recording of *Just A Minute*, I walked up the stairs of the stage and headed towards Barry Cryer. He looked at me in the way you do when you think you might know someone but cannot for the life of you remember why. I reintroduced myself and we had a chat. I showed him the book and said I was hoping to get an autograph. He could see I was nervous to approach Kenneth on my own. "Come with me" Barry said and he led me over to Kenneth. I brought out the copy of *Just Williams* and asked Kenneth if he would sign it for me. "'Ere," he said with his over exaggerated infamous nasal twang, "you're a bit previous aren't you... I didn't even know the book had come out yet. You're a bit keen" and he smiled and I was so happy. He asked what I thought of the show, I told him how much I had enjoyed it and then he reached under the table to a box and brought out a copy of a previous publication of his, Acid Drops. "Do you have this book?" he asked "No" I admitted honestly "Well then, please have this one from me." And I thanked him. And I left and literally danced all the way home.

Just A Minute returned to the BBC's Paris Studios in 1986, and I returned to watch the show too several times when I was at drama school. I would see it with a friend called Clementine. She was the niece of Clement Freud and they were known in her family as the 'Two Clemmies'. We would sit in the front row, me on occasions next to Kenneth's mother Louie. I adored being so close to Kenneth Williams and also getting the chance to see other favoured performers including actress Eleanor Summerfield and the sublime Stanley Unwin. Deep joy. We would chat with Kenneth and Clement after the show.

Nine years later and it is spring 1994. I am standing in what was Kenneth Williams' bathroom at his former flat in Osnaburgh Street, just off Great Portland Street. Kenneth had died in 1988. His flat had just been bought and was being stripped out.

Barbara Windsor and Norman Wisdom wave from the window after unveiling the Dead Comics Society plaque for Kenneth at 8 Marlborough House, 8 May 1994

Standing next to me was Barbara Windsor and Norman Wisdom. The occasion was the unveiling of a blue plaque commemorating Kenneth. In order for the press to get the shot they wanted, we needed to get Norman and Barbara looking out of the window together so they would be directly above the plaque. The problem was the window was quite high up and both Barbara and Norman were quite short (…I should talk!)

Suddenly, Barbara hoisted up her skirt and climbed on to the side of the bath. Norman climbed on to the toilet. Both leaned over and out of the window. Barbara turned round to me and said; "Morris, keep us steady please". So there I was on my knees and out of shot with my right hand on Barbara Windsor's bum and my left hand on Norman Wisdom's, in Kenneth Williams' bathroom and I remember thinking "will life ever get better than this?" And you know, to this day, I am not sure it ever has!

Kenneth Williams was warm and generous with his time. His hero status when I was growing up has remained unrivalled throughout my life.

God bless the memory of Kenneth Williams and those who seek to remember him kindly through his work, especially to the author of this book, Adam Endacott, the very finest of fans, most enthusiastic of writers and gentlest of men.

Morris Bright MBE
Borehamwood, 2021

Introduction

Not another book on Kenneth Williams I hear you say? What more can be written or seen about this unique man who was a staple part of the entertainment scene for 40 years...well...

Here is an illustrative companion to the *Companion*! For those who own a copy of *The Kenneth Williams Companion* (published in 2018) will know that 'our' Kenneth was continually working on stage, radio, film, in the recording studio and on television. This book collates together that body of work in an illustrated format and from a vast collection of photos, programmes, posters, cuttings and much more. What is presented in the following pages are a just a glimpse of materials that have been collected and curated into a chronology of Kenneth's career. The *Scrapbook* serves as a tribute to a man who remains as relevant today as he was when he died almost 35 years ago.

Since the *Companion* was published, I have had the good fortune of discovering further 'lost' footage and have uncovered even more projects that Kenneth was involved with. I hope that an updated edition of the *Companion* will appear in the near future.

The Kenneth Williams Scrapbook has been curated to sit alongside all the books on Kenneth that have gone before and I hope it is the perfect adornment for the coffee table; a volume that can be dipped in and out of whilst discovering something different on each visit to its pages.

My particular thanks go to the talented three who have provided the forewords this time, who of whom have been enthusiastic, warm and a joy to meet and speak to. Morris was superb in hosting my book launch at Elstree Studios on 15 April 2018.

A letter written by Kenneth in 1984 illustrating just some of his work on television, all detailed in the *Companion*

I wish to thank all those that have been a part of my Kenneth journey – there are countless people who have all played a different but important role in the magnificent world of 'our' Kenneth. Without one in particular though, this book wouldn't have been possible – with grateful thanks to Tim Coleman of Darkhorse Design for the design and layout – he now claims he knows more about Kenneth than I do!

Well my dearios, it just remains for me to say, sit back and enjoy looking back at a fantabulosa life!

London, September 2021

Kenneth's Family Tree

Kenneth was always keen to illustrate his family throughout his career, exclaiming that his mother, Louie, was a Morgan from Pontnewydd and his father, Charlie, from Port Talbot. However, both were born in London and the Morgan's were from Marylebone and the Williams from Cheltenham in Gloucestershire via Middlesex. Here is his immediate family, to his generation:

THE WILLIAMS FAMILY

Charles John Williams
B: 1877
D: 1931
M: 12/11/1899

Elizabeth Sarah (nee Nealon)
B: 21/07/1877
D: 16/05/1964

Charles George
B: 24/12/1899
D: 15/10/1962
M: 07/04/1925

Louisa Alexandra (nee Morgan)
B: 20/12/1901
D: 19/07/1991

George Edward
B: 1901
D: 1902

John (Jack)
B: 1903
D: unknown

Helen (Ellen)
B: 1906
D: unknown

Eliza
B: 1908
D: unknown
M: 1928

Thomas G Ward
B: 1907
D: 1933

Kenneth Charles
B: 22/02/1926
D: 15/04/1988

Alice Patricia
B: 22/04/1923
D: 07/03/1995
M: 11/08/1945

Robert Lindsay Wallace
(divorced c.1955)

THE MORGAN FAMILY

Henry Benjamin Morgan
B: 1866
D: June 1916
M: 19/06/1887

Louisa Alexandrina (nee Hoare)
B: 29/07/1868
D: 1904

M: 1911
Ellen Margaret (nee Codd)
B: 1867
D: February 1948

Lydia Jane
B: 1887
D: unknown

Henry George
B: 1889
D: 1891

Rose
B: 1891
D: unknown

Charles Victor
B: 1892
D: 1892

Alice Frances
B: 06/03/1895
D: 1981
M: 1917

William Albert Arthur
B: 20/01/1893
D: 1971

Albert W H
B: 01/02/1918
D: 07/12/1978
M: 1939

Rubina C (nee Copeland)
B: unknown
D: unknown

WAAF Corporal Pat Williams (Kenneth's sister) cuts her wedding cake with new husband, Pilot Officer Robert Lindsay Wallace from Haberfield, NSW. They were married in Christ Church, Woburn Square in 1945. Pat, a WAAF wireless operator, met Robert, an airgunner, whilst stationed in Norfolk.

| **Albert Edward** B: 21/02/1910 D: 1986 M: 1935 | **Florence Ellen (nee Crick)** B: 23/04/1911 D: 09/07/1990 | **Ivy** B: 1913 D: unknown | **Francis H** B: 1914 D: 1915 | **Phyllis** B: 18/01/1917 D: 2002 M: 1941 | **Frank Eric Edward Gidley** B: 05/09/1919 D: 25/01/1980 | **Stanley** B: 08/09/1919 D: 2005 | **Leonard** B: 1922 D: 1922 |

| **Florence** B: 1943 | **Geoffrey** B: 1947 | **Laurence G** B: 1948 | **Paul** B: 1950 |

| **Henry Frederick James** B: 1897 D: 01/02/1952 M: 1922 | **Elizabeth Annie (nee Neal)** B: 1897 D: 06/07/1978 | **Edith Louise** B: 04/09/1899 D: 27/12/1982 M: 1926 | **Siegfried Henry Kaufmann** B: 23/10/1892 D: 06/03/1982 | **Louisa Alexandra** | **Daisy** B: 1904 D: 27/07/1959 M: 1930 | **Clifford Hickman** B: 09/04/1904 D: 1995 |

| **Eva Joy** B: 1928 D: 05/05/2014 M: 1958 | **Michael Hewett Colyer** B: 18/09/1922 D: 16/02/2016 |

| **Frederick Ronald** B: 21/04/1921 D: 1990 M: 1945 | **Iris Lilian (nee Pearce)** B: 21/12/1924 D: 2005 | **Joan W** B: 16/07/1922 D: 31/01/2021 M: 1942 | **Patrick A Dunbar** B: 1915 D: 2000 |

Kenneth Charles Williams was born on 22 February 1926 at 14:30 at home in the upstairs bedroom of 11 Bingfield Street in Islington. The first born child for Louisa (Louie) and Charles (Charlie) Williams and a step brother for Alice (known as Pat).

At the age of nine, in 1935, Kenneth made his theatrical debut as Princess Angelica in *The Rose and the Ring*. Pictured here on the roof of Manchester Street Junior Boys' School, it was his first role in drag and his performance was a firm favourite with the audience.

No. 14747886: Williams KC, Private (later Sergeant). Kenneth commenced his career in the army as a lithographer in Survey Section Royal Engineers in 1944. He was then shipped to the Hydrographic Section at Dehra Dun, India in 1945 and thence to Kandy, Ceylon on the occasion of the Japanese Peace Treaty.

Combined Services Entertainment (CSE), No.1 British Transit Camp, Nee Soon Singapore

July-October 1947 – *At Your Service* – a new revue devised by Albert Arlen. The opening number, *We're Men of the Service* is illustrated here. "We all wore navy-blue battledress, with three yellow tapes, and yellow trousers" remembered Stanley Baxter (fourth from left) and Kenneth is first left.

The company of *At Your Service*, including Rae Hammond, Stanley Baxter, Kenneth (front row, middle) and Peter Nichols (back row, extreme right).

Combined Services Entertainment presents "AT YOUR SERVICE" A SIDE-SPLITTING REVUE

with

Ken Williams — Stan Baxter
Geoffrey Deakin — Dave Perton
Lawrie Clayton — Rae Hammond
Brian Hargreaves — Les Wilson
Ray Ashley — Colin Maynard
Peter Nichols,
AND
LEO CONRICHE
AT THE PIANO

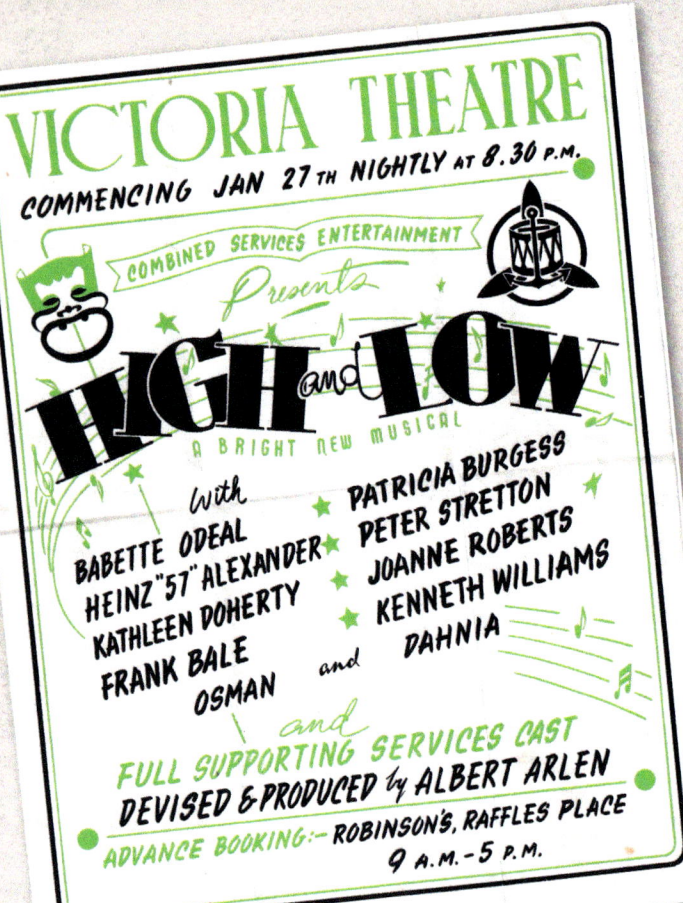

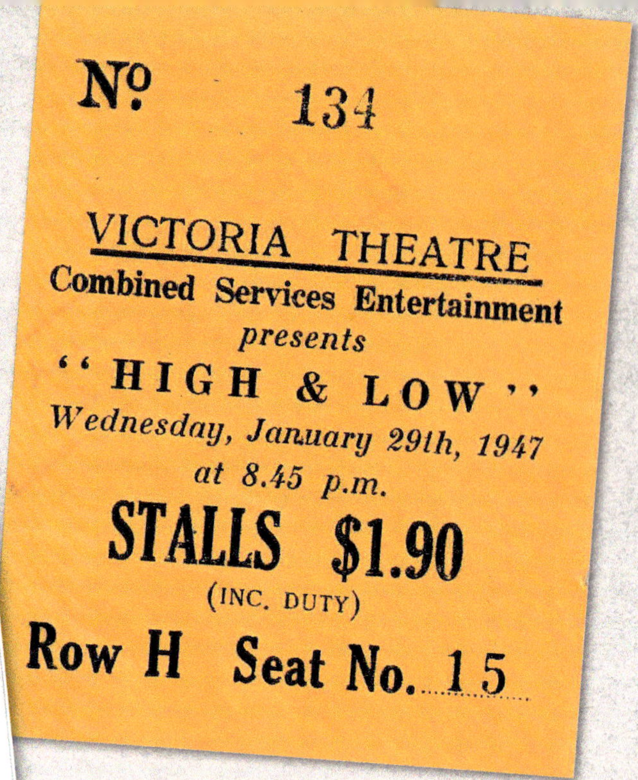

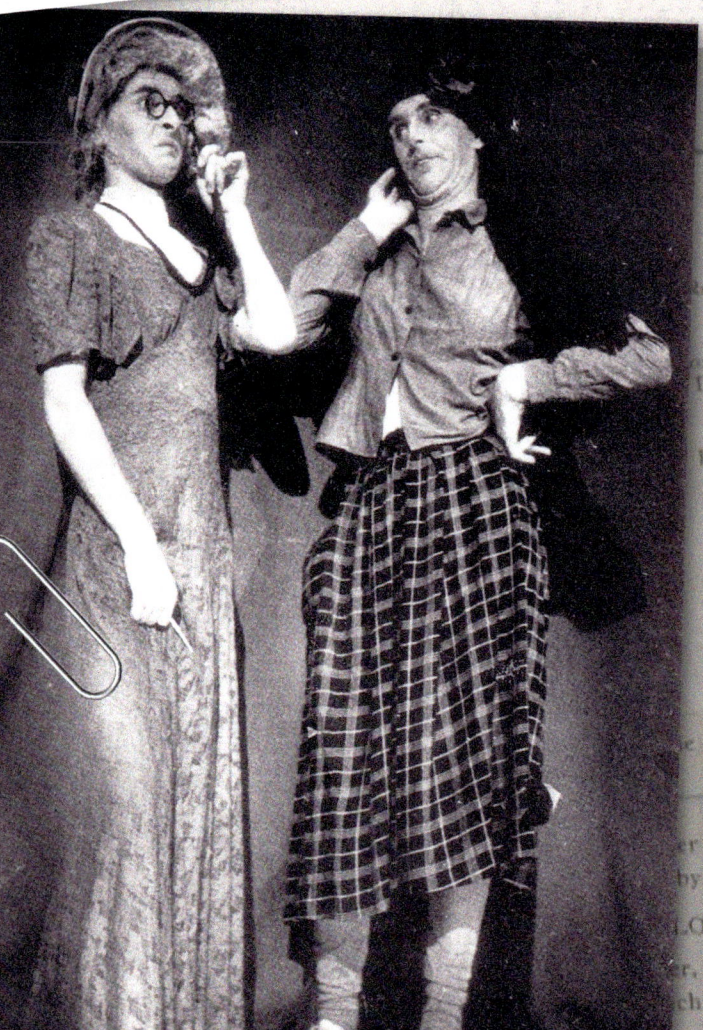

High and Low, January/February 1947, Victoria Theatre, Singapore. A bright new musical devised by Albert Arlen. Kenneth is pictured (left) as Eva Tassle with Peter Stretton as Lillian Mawdsley in the sketch entitled *Cat's Cradle*.

(10)

FRANK B
many f
our first
recall h
which w
hails fro
his brig
is typica
this ne
Arlen
lasge p
tackled

It won't
returns
and leav
he reach
have wi
favourite
it will
chips, c
tripe ren
intends
the lesse
to the "
Busy er
tour star
keep up
occupatio

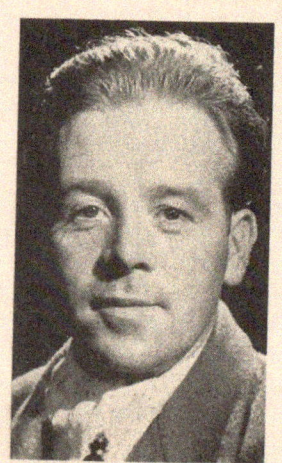

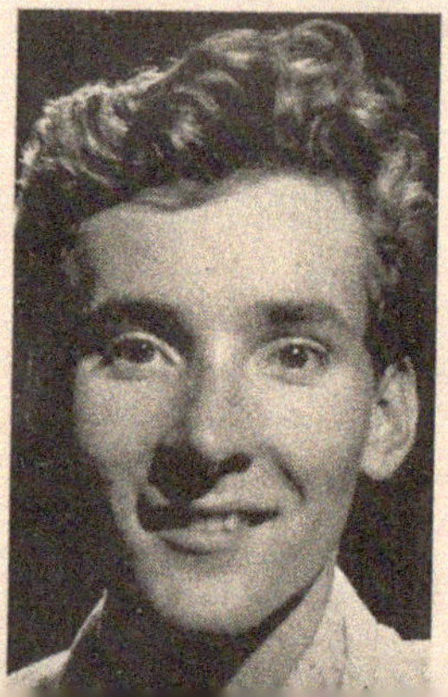

KENNETH
from the
Engineer
Photo W
much int
spare tim
his own
perience
for mim
to his
acting
in London before joining the army. Ken applied to join CSE from Ceylon and after a few weeks of weary wa'ting was posted to the production centre where he went into "Seven Keys to Baldpate" taking the part of the harassed aetective. In this new production he has quite a variety of characters to portray.

Rather in contrast to his "public" demeanour Ken's private life revolves mostly around books and 'charpoys.' He finds the combina-

oy Lees and Bunny Reynolds.

anne Roberts, Kathleen Doherty & John McKenna.

Patricia Burgess & the Boys of High and Low.

Frank Bale
Maurice Weintroub
Kenneth Williams

e full company

er at the Piano
by Barri Chat

LOW" BAND,
er, Johnny Brown, Bill Lake,
chards, John Edwards.

DEVISED AND PRODUCED
BY
ALBERT ARLEN

NEWQUAY REPERTORY PLAYERS
TELEPHONE 3379

Monday, 23rd August. For Six Nights, at 8.30 p.m.

"The Sacred Flame"
A play in Three Acts, by SOMERSET MAUGHAM.
Characters in order of appearance:

Maurice Tabret	Frederick Treves
Dr. Harvester	Kenneth Williams
Mrs. Tabret	Sara Jameson
Nurse Wayland	Linda Hayward
Alice	Rosemary Mathews
Major Liconda	Peter Ashby-Bailey
Stella	Joan Dale
Colin Tabret	Gordon Pearce

The action of the play ... ... Mrs. Tabret's residence, near London

Lessee ... RONALD BRAND...
Business Manager...
Stage Managers...
Assistant Stage M...

Scenery Painted...

Next...

Morning Coffee
Lunches - Teas
Suppers
to 11 p.m.

1948 – A fresh faced Kenneth (far right) in Newquay with fellow actor Peter Ashby-Bailey, with whom he shared a room, and Mrs Merrifield and her family, their landlady at 7a Bank Street.

NEWQUAY REPERTORY PLAYERS

The Company of Three presents Newquay Repertory Players, Newquay Theatre, Cornwall.

1948 – Kenneth's professional debut as an actor, at the age of 22, as Ninian Fraser in *The First Mrs Fraser*.

COSY NOOK THEATRE
NEWQUAY 3365

RONALD BRANDON and DICKIE POUNDS
in conjunction with RONNIE HILL
PRESENT

"OUT OF THE BLUE"
The Sparkling Summer Show.

Weekdays   Prices: 5/-, 3/3 & 1/10   All Seats Bookable
at 8.30 p.m.

"OUT OF THE BLUE" THE COSY REVUE

A. E. Jenkin & Son
24, EAST STREET,
NEWQUAY.

Phone 2073 for the best
LADIES' and GENT'S
HAIRDRESSERS
in NEWQUAY

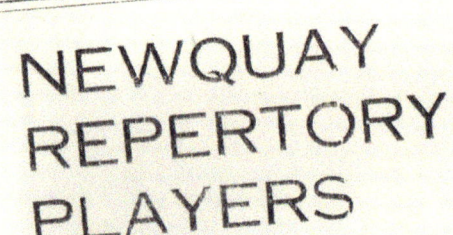

NEWQUAY REPERTORY PLAYERS
TELEPHONE 3379

Monday, 9th August.   For Six Nights, at 8.30 p.m.

"JUPITER LAUGHS"

A play in Three Acts by A. J. CRONIN.

Characters in order of appearance:

Edgar Bragg, Medical Superintendent of Hopewell Towers	Stanley Hildebrandt
Gladys Bragg (His Wife)	Sara Jameson
Paul Venner, Assistant Physician at Hopewell Towers	John Field
Richard Drewett ,, ,, ,, ,, ,,	Peter Ashby-Bailey
George Thorogood ,, ,, ,, ,, ,,	Frederick Treves
Mary Murray ,, ,, ,, ,, ,,	Joan Dale
Fanny Leeming, Matron at Hopewell Towers	Rosemary Mathews
Jennie, Maid at Hopewell Towers	Sonia Moray
Albert Chivers, District Representative of Glysters Ltd.	Kenneth Williams
Martha Fo...	

The Poltergeist, August 1948, Kenneth (2nd right) as Vincent Ebury with the cast in Frank Harvey's three-act play.

NEWQUAY REPERTORY PLAYERS
TELEPHONE 3379

Monday, 13th September.   For Six Nights, at 8.30 p.m.

"The Importance of being Earnest"

by OSCAR WILDE.

A trivial Comedy for serious people.

Played for the first time at the St. James' Theatre on Thursday, February 14th, 1895.

Characters in order of appearance:

Lane (Mr. Moncrieff's man-servant)	Stanley Hildebrandt
Algernon Moncrieff	Kenneth Williams

Repertory theatre was a part of Kenneth's early career for six years, illustrated here is his time in Margate, spring 1950.

Kenneth's radio debut, on the BBC Light Programme, was in 1949 in *Gordon Grantley KC*, his second appearance is shown here in the episode *Patent Pending*.

A selection of posters from Kenneth's time at the Devonshire Park Theatre in Eastbourne including his debut performance on 13 February 1950 as Danny in *Night Must Fall*. It was here he met Michael Anderson, who would become Kenneth's agent in 1981.

'The Land of My Fathers' Pageant Play of Wales was a unique and colourful pageant play, specifically devised to celebrate the Festival of Britain year, telling the story of Wales through the ages. Kenneth appeared in six scenes.

"The Land of my Fathers"

PAGEANT PLAY OF WALES

SOPHIA GARDENS PAVILION
CARDIFF

JULY 30—AUGUST 11
1951

PROGRAMME SIXPENCE

FESTIVAL OF BRITAIN
WELSH COMMITTEE

THE PAGEANT PLAY COMMITTEE

presents

"The Land of my Fathers"
A PAGEANT PLAY OF WALES

by

CLIFFORD EVANS
JACK JONES   RICHARD VAUGHAN
DAVID MONGER   KEN ETHERIDGE
A. G. PRYS-JONES   A. J. RODERICK

DEVISED AND DIRECTED BY
CLIFFORD EVANS

HISTORICAL ADVISER
PROFESSOR WILLIAM REES, M.A., D.Sc., F.R.Hist.S., F.S.A.

With Music by ARWEL HUGHES

SOPHIA GARDENS PAVILION, CARDIFF
July 30—August 11, 1951

GEOFFREY CURTIS

RICHARD BEBB

KENNETH WILLIAMS

DAVID MORRELL

FREDERIC STEGER

JOHN BARKER

Page eleven

THE CAST
PART I
PROLOGUE

The Narrator . . . . DONALD HOUSTON

The Chairman
Monmouth . . . . Peter Edwards
Merioneth . . . . Edward Macarthy
Radnor . . . . D. J. Morgan
Brecon . . . . W. R. Chappell
Cardigan . . . . John Barry
Glamorgan . . . . Haydn Davies
Carmarthen . . . . Roy Cambrian
Flint . . . . Percy Keats
Caernarvon . . . . Glyn James
Pembroke . . . . W. J. Davies
Denbigh . . . . Sulwen Morgan
Anglesey . . . . Peter Colquhoun
                                         Miss R. Evens

SCENE 1. THE DEATH OF ARTHUR

King Arthur . . . . Geoffrey Curtis
Sir Bedivere . . . . David Morrell
Barbarian . . . . Clayton Thatcher
Queens . . . . . . Iwana Jones, Patricia Evans, Pamela Curtis
Romans . . . Ivor Jones, Gwyn Beard, Trevor Matthews, Russell Bennett,
               Walter Williams, C. F. Warren, L. W. Prosser

SCENE 2. THE CONVERSION OF BOIA

St. David . . . . Harold Lewis
Boia . . . . Clayton Thatcher
Boia's son . . . . Digby Day
Servant . . . . Henry Davies
Two boys . . . . George Baldwin, Alun Baldwin

SCENE 3. THE MAKING OF THE LAWS

Hywel Dda . . . . Peter Gyngell
The Bishop . . . . Frederic Steger
Blegywryd . . . . Kenneth Williams
Scribe . . . . Thomas Fawcett
Siôn . . . . John Barry
Siân . . . . Sulwen Morgan

SCENE 4. THE PROPHECY OF THE OLD MAN OF PENCADER

Henry II . . . . Richard Bebb
Old Man of Pencader . . . . Peter Edwards

Page four

Kenneth featured in production photos from his final repertory theatre, The Bridgwater Repertory Company, in May-June 1954.

3 February 1952, *The Wonderful Visit*, Kenneth's television debut as The Angel. ▼

Released in 1953, Kenneth as Jack, the pot boy, with Sir Laurence Olivier in *The Beggar's Opera*, his first film in colour. ▶

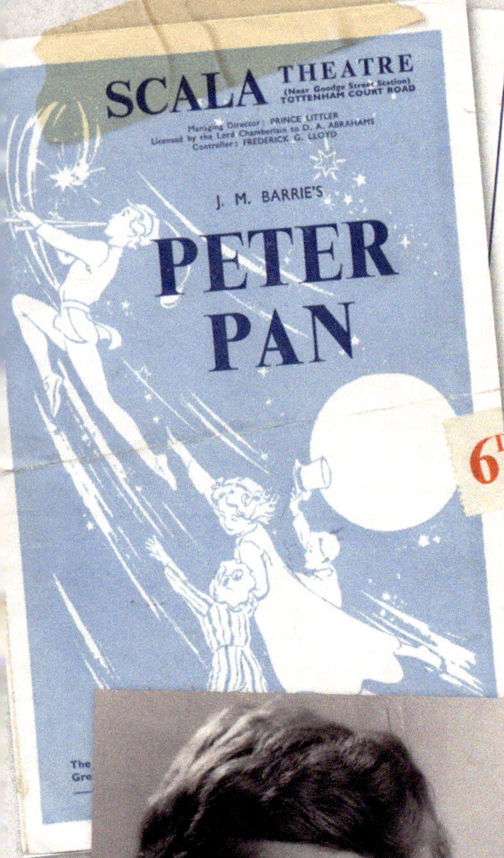

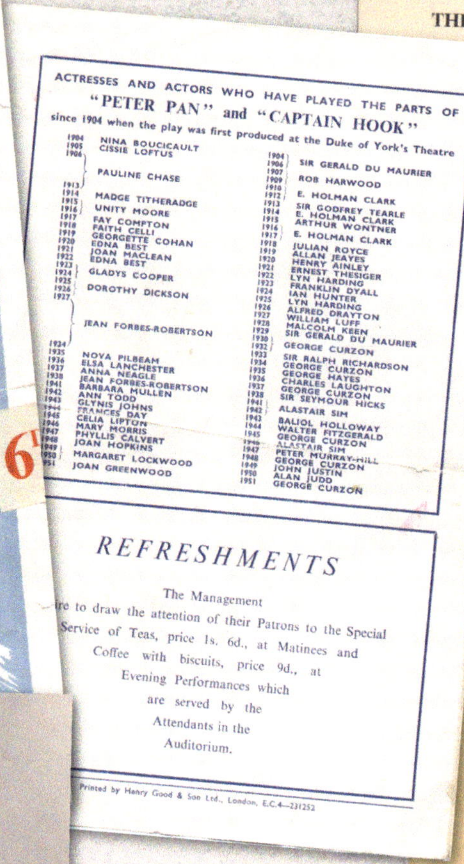

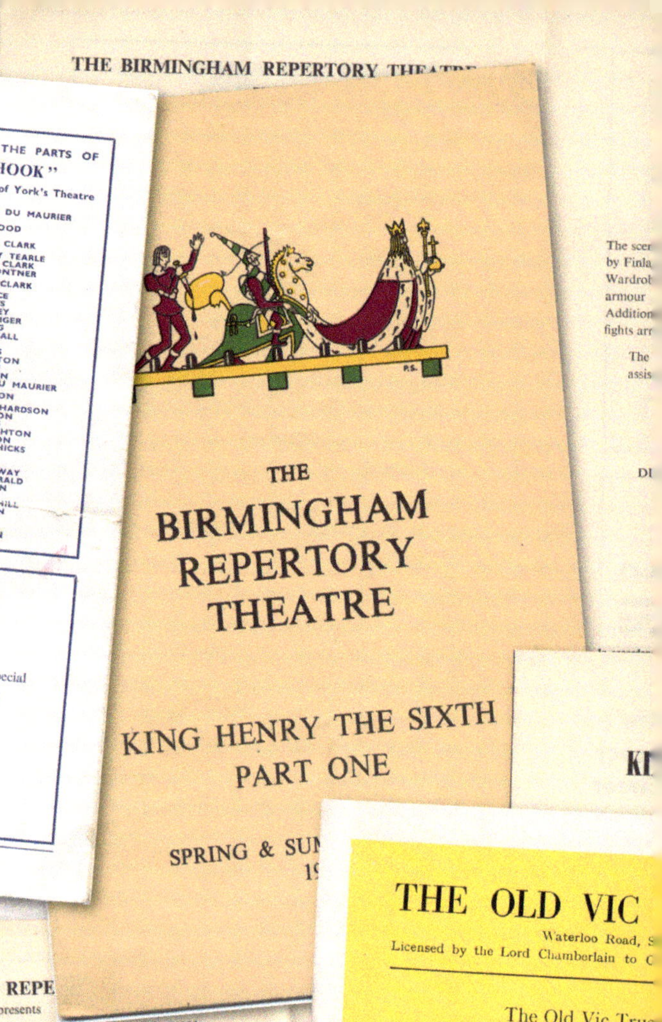

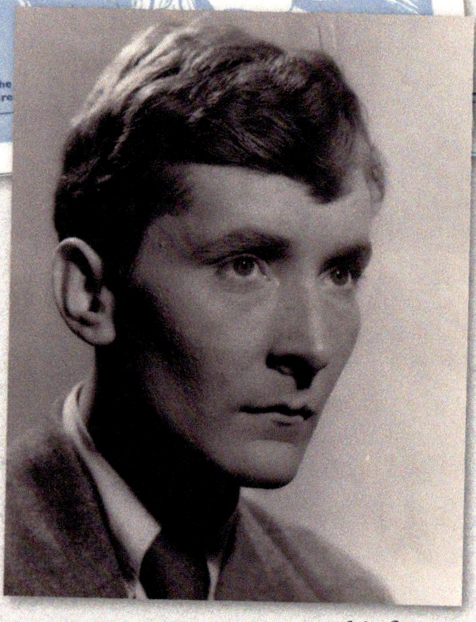

1952-53, *Peter Pan* was Kenneth's first touring production from London via the provincial cities and ending in Bristol. He played the character of Slightly.

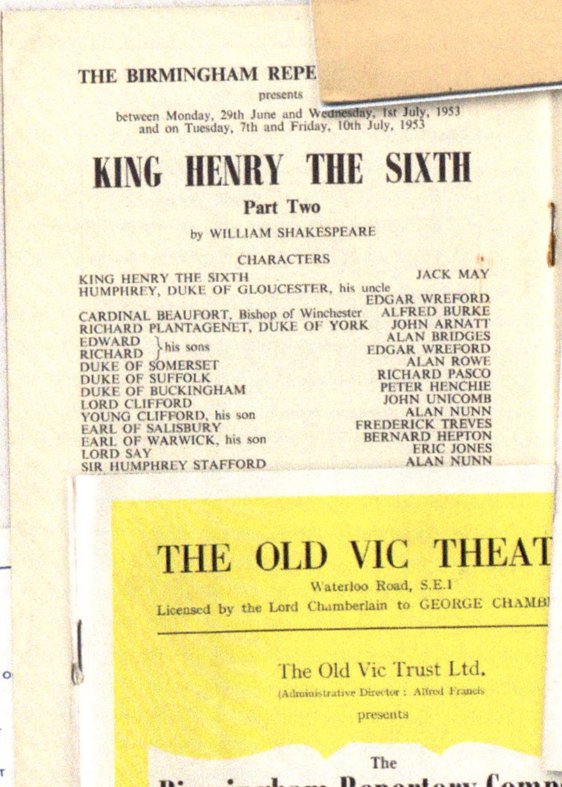

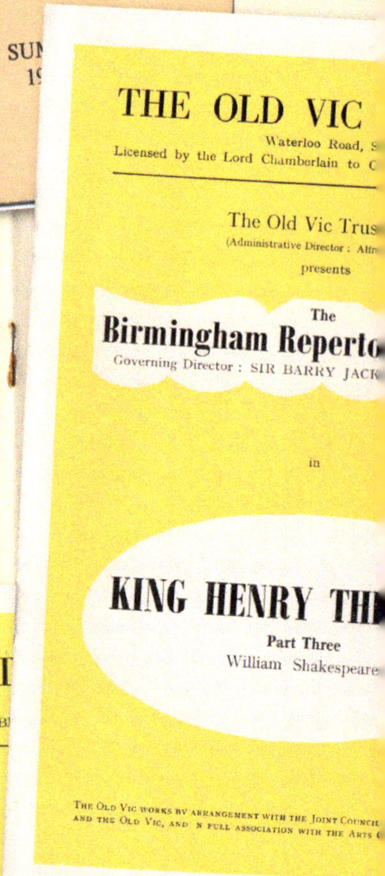

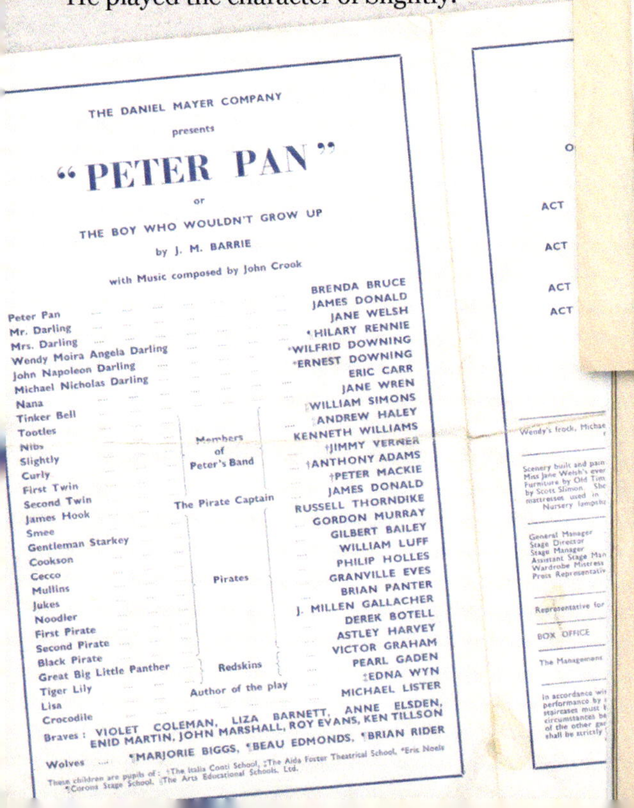

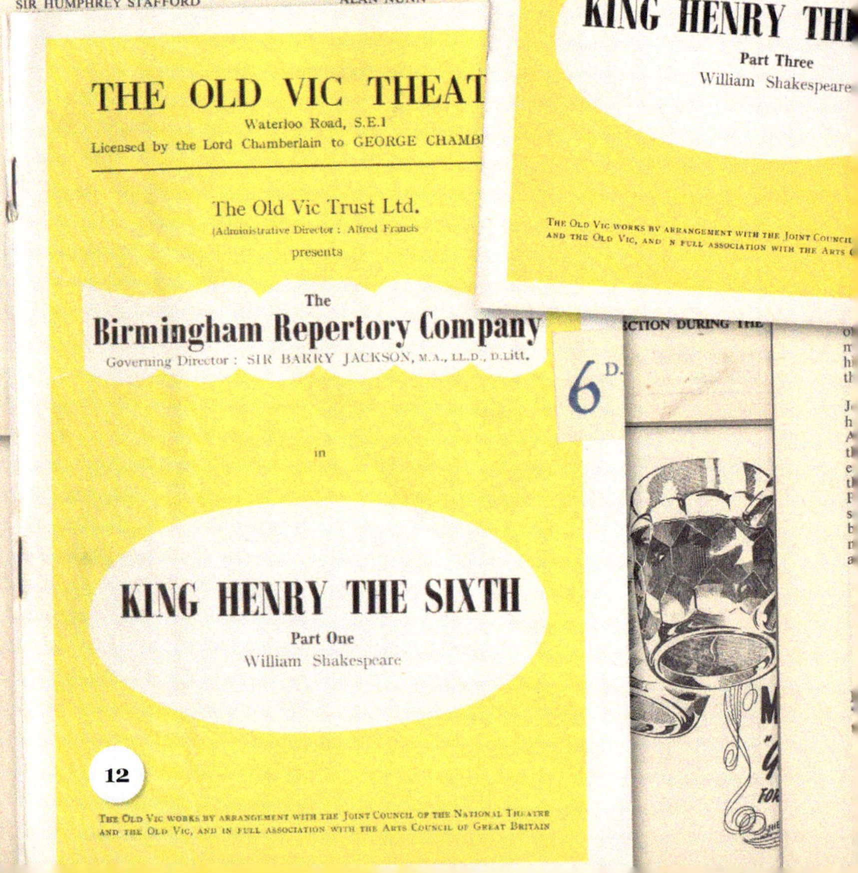

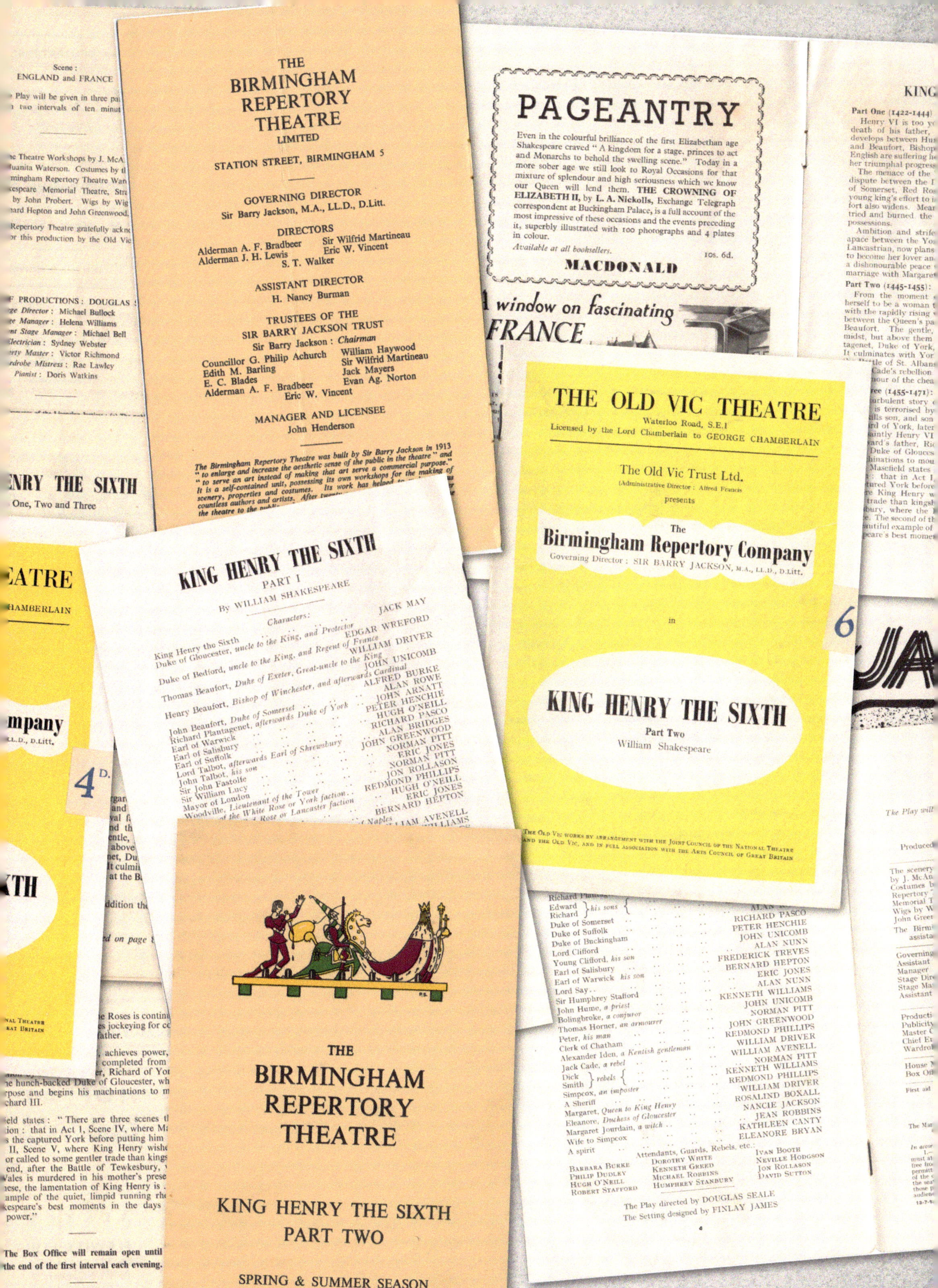

THE BIRMINGHAM REPERTORY THEATRE LIMITED

STATION STREET, BIRMINGHAM 5

GOVERNING DIRECTOR
Sir Barry Jackson, M.A., LL.D., D.Litt.

DIRECTORS
Alderman A. F. Bradbeer, Sir Wilfrid Martineau
Alderman J. H. Lewis, Eric W. Vincent
S. T. Walker

ASSISTANT DIRECTOR
H. Nancy Burman

TRUSTEES OF THE SIR BARRY JACKSON TRUST
Sir Barry Jackson : *Chairman*
Councillor G. Philip Achurch, William Haywood
Edith M. Barling, Sir Wilfrid Martineau
E. C. Blades, Jack Mayers
Alderman A. F. Bradbeer, Evan Ag. Norton
Eric W. Vincent

MANAGER AND LICENSEE
John Henderson

The Birmingham Repertory Theatre was built by Sir Barry Jackson in 1913 "to enlarge and increase the aesthetic sense of the public in the theatre" and "to serve an art instead of making that art serve a commercial purpose." It is a self-contained unit, possessing its own workshops for the making of scenery, properties and costumes. Its work has helped ... countless authors and artists. After ...

PAGEANTRY

Even in the colourful brilliance of the first Elizabethan age Shakespeare craved "A kingdom for a stage, princes to act and Monarchs to behold the swelling scene." Today in a more sober age we still look to Royal Occasions for that mixture of splendour and high seriousness which we know our Queen will lend them. **THE CROWNING OF ELIZABETH II**, by **L. A. Nickolls**, Exchange Telegraph correspondent at Buckingham Palace, is a full account of the most impressive of these occasions and the events preceding it, superbly illustrated with 100 photographs and 4 plates in colour.

Available at all booksellers. 10s. 6d.

MACDONALD

A window on fascinating FRANCE

THE OLD VIC THEATRE
Waterloo Road, S.E.1
Licensed by the Lord Chamberlain to GEORGE CHAMBERLAIN

The Old Vic Trust Ltd.
(Administrative Director : Alfred Francis)
presents

The Birmingham Repertory Company
Governing Director : SIR BARRY JACKSON, M.A., LL.D., D.Litt.

in

KING HENRY THE SIXTH
Part Two
William Shakespeare

THE OLD VIC WORKS BY ARRANGEMENT WITH THE JOINT COUNCIL OF THE NATIONAL THEATRE AND THE OLD VIC, AND IN FULL ASSOCIATION WITH THE ARTS COUNCIL OF GREAT BRITAIN

KING HENRY THE SIXTH
PART I
By WILLIAM SHAKESPEARE

Characters:

King Henry the Sixth	JACK MAY
Duke of Gloucester, *uncle to the King, and Protector*	EDGAR WREFORD
Duke of Bedford, *uncle to the King, and Regent of France*	WILLIAM DRIVER
Thomas Beaufort, *Duke of Exeter, Great-uncle to the King*	JOHN UNICOMB
Henry Beaufort, *Bishop of Winchester, and afterwards Cardinal*	ALFRED BURKE
John Beaufort, *Duke of Somerset*	ALAN ROWE
Richard Plantagenet, *afterwards Duke of York*	JOHN ARNATT
Earl of Warwick	PETER HENCHIE
Earl of Salisbury	HUGH O'NEILL
Earl of Suffolk	RICHARD PASCO
Lord Talbot, *afterwards Earl of Shrewsbury*	ALAN BRIDGES
John Talbot, *his son*	JOHN GREENWOOD
Sir John Fastolfe	NORMAN PITT
Sir William Lucy	ERIC JONES
Mayor of London	NORMAN PITT
Woodville, *Lieutenant of the Tower*	JON ROLLASON
... *of the White Rose or York faction*	REDMOND PHILLIPS
... *Rose or Lancaster faction*	HUGH O'NEILL
	ERIC JONES
	BERNARD HEPTON
... *Naples*	WILLIAM AVENELL

THE BIRMINGHAM REPERTORY THEATRE

KING HENRY THE SIXTH
PART TWO

SPRING & SUMMER SEASON
1953

Edward } *his sons*	
Richard }	RICHARD PASCO
Duke of Somerset	PETER HENCHIE
Duke of Suffolk	JOHN UNICOMB
Duke of Buckingham	ALAN NUNN
Lord Clifford	FREDERICK TREVES
Young Clifford, *his son*	BERNARD HEPTON
Earl of Salisbury	ERIC JONES
Earl of Warwick *his son*	ALAN NUNN
Lord Say	KENNETH WILLIAMS
Sir Humphrey Stafford	JOHN UNICOMB
John Hume, *a priest*	NORMAN PITT
Bolingbroke, *a conjuror*	JOHN GREENWOOD
Thomas Horner, *an armourer*	REDMOND PHILLIPS
Peter, *his man*	WILLIAM DRIVER
Clerk of Chatham	WILLIAM AVENELL
Alexander Iden, *a Kentish gentleman*	NORMAN PITT
Jack Cade, *a rebel*	KENNETH WILLIAMS
Dick } *rebels*	REDMOND PHILLIPS
Smith }	WILLIAM DRIVER
Simpcox, *an imposter*	ROSALIND BOXALL
A Sheriff	NANCIE JACKSON
Margaret, *Queen to King Henry*	JEAN ROBBINS
Eleanore, *Duchess of Gloucester*	KATHLEEN CANTY
Margaret Jourdain, *a witch*	ELEANORE BRYAN
Wife to Simpcox	
A spirit	

Attendants, Guards, Rebels, etc.:
BARBARA BURKE, PHILIP DUDLEY, HUGH O'NEILL, ROBERT STAFFORD, DOROTHY WHITE, KENNETH GREED, MICHAEL ROBBINS, HUMPHREY STANBURY, IVAN BOOTH, NEVILLE HODGSON, JON ROLLASON, DAVID SUTTON

The Play directed by DOUGLAS SEALE
The Setting designed by FINLAY JAMES

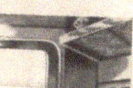

June-July 1953, The Birmingham Repertory Company was the first to perform Shakespeare's *King Henry the Sixth Parts One, Two and Three* in its entirety since Sir Frank Benson at the time. The productions were then staged at The Old Vic Theatre.

SAINT JOAN
by
BERNARD SHAW

Characters in the order of their appearance:

Robert de Baudricourt	KEVIN STONEY
Steward	DESMOND JORDAN
Joan	SIOBHAN McKENNA
Archbishop of Rheims	FRANK ROYDE
Bertrand de Poulengey	BARRY CASSIN
Monseigneur de la Tremouille	WILLIAM ABNEY
Court Page	TOMMY MOORE
Gilles de Rais	SEYMOUR GREEN
Captain de la Hire	JOSEPH CHELTON
The Dauphin (later Charles VII)	KENNETH WILLIAMS
Duchesse de la Tremouille	ROWENA INGRAM
Lady in Waiting	BARBARA LYNNE
Dunois, Bastard of Orleans	PETER WYNGARDE
Dunois' Page	DAVID SAIRE
Richard Beauchamp, Earl of Warwick	DOUGLAS WILMER
Chaplain de Stogumber	DAVID MARCH
Peter Cauchon, Bishop of Beauvais	OLIVER BURT
Warwick's Page	TOMMY MOORE
The Inquisitor	CHARLES LLOYD PACK
Canon d'Estivet	SEYMOUR GREEN
Canon de Courcelles	WILLIAM ABNEY
Brother Martin Ladvenu	DESMOND JORDAN
Executioner	BARRY CASSIN
English Soldier	BARRY LOWE
Gentleman	KEVIN STONEY

Tommy Moore appears by arrangement with the Corona Stage School.

THE ARTS THEATRE

Theatre Director: John
General Manager: Joan R

presents

SAINT JOAN

by

Bernard Shaw

PRICE SIXPE

ARTS THEATRE
"SAINT JOAN"
By BERNARD SHAW

The memorable performances of Dame Sybil Thorndike and certain of her successors in the name part of this great play should not be allowed to blind one to the fact that the play as a whole is greater than the part, and that Shaw saw to it that the part itself was actress-proof. It is not even a part, perhaps, of which it is possible to vary the reading. All that can be done is to increase the power of the performance. Yet although no actress can altogether fail as Saint Joan, this does not mean that she automatically succeeds as her. It is one thing not to ruin the play, a contingency against which Shaw effectually provided. It is altogether another so to vitalize and transfigure the character that it transcends in its simplicity the complicated and sophisticated personages about it whose mental and moral processes are so fascinating to follow—that, in short, it makes us believe in Joan as a worker of apparent miracles.

The latest Joan happens to be an Irish one, which is an interesting reminder that the original creator of Saint Joan, in New York, was also an Irish actress, but does not alter the fundamental question: will she add to the power of the play? The most striking quality of Miss Siobhan McKenna's performance is its sincerity, which almost overcomes the occasional handicap of costumes that recall Peter Pan and lends pathos to the rather waif-like figure with its cropped hair. Her best scene is her first, perhaps because she is not then dressed like Peter Pan and has therefore not to combat in her audience an entirely different association; and at the beginning of the trial one is moved by the spectacle of such evident misery.

Of the other performances few are such as to challenge our recollections of their predecessors. Mr. Douglas Wilmer's Warwick, Mr. Oliver Burt's Cauchon, and Mr. Peter Wyngarde's Dunois, however, are all serviceable.

1954-55, *Saint Joan*, the turning point in Kenneth's career and his first time in London's West End appearing as the Dauphin, later Charles VII. A total of 39 performances at The Arts Theatre Club and 125 performances at St Martin's Theatre.

14

ST. MARTIN'S THEATRE

WEST STREET, CAMBRIDGE CIRCUS, W.C.2

Licensee: J. M. Cook   Lessees: BRIGHT ENTERPRISES LTD.
Managing Directors: J. M. COOK & A. M. COOK   Tel. TEM. BAR 1443

HENRY SHEREK

presents

SIOBHAN McKENNA

in

Saint Joan

by

BERNARD SHAW

ST. MARTIN'S THEATRE

WEST STREET, CAMBRIDGE CIRCUS, W.C.2

Licensee: J. M. Cook   Lessees: Bright Enterprises Ltd.
Managing Directors: J. M. Cook and A. M. Cook   Temple Bar 1443

Evenings at 7.30   **Tuesday and Saturday at 2.30**

HENRY SHEREK presents

SIOBHAN McKENNA
in
SAINT JOAN
by BERNARD SHAW

DOUGLAS WILMER
FRANK ROYDE
DAVID MARCH
SEYMOUR GREEN
KENNETH WILLIAMS
BARRY LOWE
STEWART WELLER
DAVID HIGSON

OLIVER BURT
KEVIN STONEY
PETER WHITBREAD
DESMOND JORDAN
ROBERT CARTLAND
EDMUND GRAY
ROWENA INGRAM
DAVID SAIRE

CHARLES LLOYD PACK

DIRECTED BY JOHN FERNALD

Settings by PAUL MAYO
Costumes by Michael Ellis

Stalls 15/-, 12/6; Dress Circle 14/6, 10/6; Upper Circle 7/6, 4/6

THE WORLD OF THE THEATRE

PRINCESS AND SAINT

By J. C. TREWIN

"BERNARD SHAW'S 'SAINT JOAN' AT THE ARTS: A SCENE IN THE CATHEDRAL OF RHEIMS AFTER JOAN (SIOBHAN McKENNA) HAS BEEN CROWNED WITH (L. TO R.) CAPTAIN DE LA HIRE (JOSEPH CHELTON); DUNOIS (PETER WYNGARDE); JOAN (SIOBHAN McKENNA); THE ARCHBISHOP OF RHEIMS (FRANK ROYDE); NOW CHARLES VII. (KENNETH WILLIAMS) AND GILLES DE RAIS (SEYMOUR GREEN)."

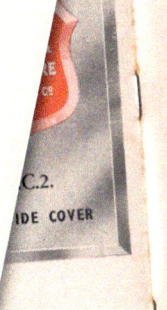

KENNETH WILLIAMS,
ST. MARCHMONT STREET,
LONDON, W.C.1
TERMINUS 4870.

24th February 1955.

Dear Sir,

It was kind of you to write of your reactions to this production of SAINT JOAN — and other members of the cast were heartened to learn about such favourable comment.

I think that I have covered everybody in the autograph business — I went round all the dressing rooms.

yours sincerely,

Kenneth

Hancock's Half Hour, Kenneth was part of the team from its first broadcast on 2 November 1954 through to Series 6 and the episode *The Childhood Sweetheart*; recording a total of 90 episodes. He played a variety of parts across his five year association, many in what would become known as the 'Snide' character. He is seen here with Tony Hancock, Sidney James, Bill Kerr and Hattie Jacques.

June-July 1955, *Moby Dick* was an open-stage production with no scenery and Orson Welles' own adaptation of Herman Melville's novel. Such was the impact of working with Welles, Kenneth would include a story about the production in almost every chat show appearance.

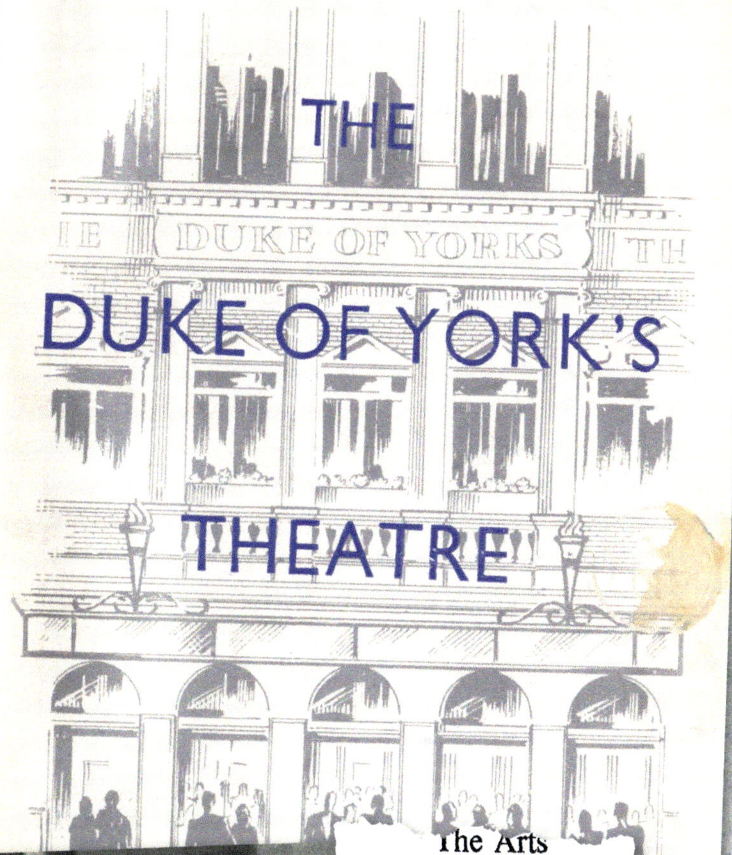

Duke of York's Theatre
ST MARTINS LANE WC 2 Tel: TEM 5122
Managing Agents: Theatre Managers Ltd
Licenced by the Lord Chamberlain to E. W. Crossley Taylor

OSCAR LEWENSTEIN AND WOLF MANKOWITZ
in association with
MARTIN GABEL AND HENRY MARGOLIS
present

ORSON WELLES
in his own play
MOBY DICK
adapted from the novel by
HERMAN MELVILLE
with
GORDON JACKSON
Kenneth Williams   Peter Sallis   We...
Joan Plowright   Jefferson Clifford
John Boyd Brent   Joseph Ch...
and
PATRICK McGOOHAN
Associate Producer William Cha...
Music specially composed by Antho...
The Play staged by Mr. Wel...

From 16th June for 4 we...
Monday to Friday 7.30 pm   Saturday 5.3...

ASSISTANT STAGE MANAGER
(afterwards "Tashtego" & "Captain of the Rachel")

A STAGE HAND WITH AN HARMONICA
(afterwards "Portuguese Sailor" and "Dagoo"...

OTHER STAGE HANDS

A MIDDLE-AGED ACTOR (afterwards "Stubb")
AN EXPERIENCED ACTOR
(afterwards "Peleg" and "Old Cornish Sailor") JEFFERSON CLIFFORD
A SERIOUS ACTOR (afterwards "Starbuck") ... PATRICK McGOOHAN
A VERY SERIOUS ACTOR (afterwards "Elijah"
"Ship's Carpenter" "Old Bedford Sailor" and others) KENNETH WILLIAMS
AN ACTOR MANAGER
(afterwards "Father Mapple" and "Ahab") ... ORSON WELLES

Associate Producer WILLIAM CHAPPELL
Music Composed by ANTHONY COLLINS
Stage Decorations by MARY OWEN

Musical Effects by Richard Johnson and T. Blades

THE DUKE OF YORK'S THEATRE

The Arts
DUKE OF YORK'S THEATRE
"MOBY DICK"
By ORSON WELLES
(From the novel by HERMAN MELVILLE)

Ishmael	GORDON JACKSON
Pip	JOAN PLOWRIGHT
Flask	PETER SALLIS
Bo'sun	JOHN GRAY
Tashtego	JOHN BOYD-BRENT
Dagoo	JOSEPH CHELTON
Stubb	WENSLEY PITHEY
Peleg	JEFFERSON CLIFFORD
Starbuck	PATRICK McGOOHAN
Elijah	KENNETH WILLIAMS
Ahab	ORSON WELLES

Produced by ORSON WELLES

The theatre, for Mr. Orson Welles, is an adventure; and to an adventurer so valiant our hearts go out even when he comes to wreck.

He sets out this time to hammer into some sort of stage shape what is perhaps the greatest of sea stories; and he is quite well aware that he has to reckon not only with a vast and elaborate account of the hunting of a mighty and mysterious whale but with an account of the mysterious and troubled soul of Herman Melville. Everything is against him, Melville's language which he tries in vain to versify, the symbols which lose their way amid the traffic of the stage, the absence of Melville's sea and the absence of the whale. Yet for a while, for something like half the performance, he succeeds against all reasonable expectation.

His plan is to present a madly impossible stage representation of Melville's novel as an indifferent company of American actors at the turn of the century are rehearsing it on an empty stage and in any old clothes. The ship sails in search of a single whale and the character of the tough, resolute and heroic Ahab is established well enough by the conflict between him and Starbuck, who holds stubbornly that it is wrong to mark down one whale for destruction simply for the sake of vengeance. Starbuck is overborne by the old man's unshakable strength of purpose. Our interest thus secured is turned to excitement by the simple device of lowering from the flies a dense tangle of ropes with here and there a spar. By their play with the ropes and with the appropriate lurchings the company carry us with them through a terrific typhoon, and the curtain is brought down with a remarkably well contrived scene of Ahab infecting the crew with his own rage to kill the whale.

The interval finds the audience a little dizzy, almost perhaps to the point of sea-sickness, but afterwards the temperature falls and Mr. Welles's adventure is clearly making for the rocks. He finds no satisfactory way to indicate that the whale represents vast and mystically apprehended forces at enmity with all human ideals. His scattered hints do not suffice to bring home to us the truth that it is Ahab's lucifer-like pride, as much as the awful power of the whale, which foredooms the champion of mankind to destruction. And the attempt to stage the fight with the whale fails pathetically. It is like nursery heroics taken altogether too seriously. Yet when all is said and done the evening, though most exhausting, has been worth having.

Mr. Welles himself plays Ahab. As an actor he has an impressive voice and an impressive face, but neither the voice nor the face is particularly expressive

LYRIC THEATRE — HAMMERSMITH

Lessees: Associated Theatre Seasons Ltd.   Licensee: J. Baxter Somerville
Telephone: Riverside 4412

THURSDAY, SEPTEMBER 8th, 1955, at 7.30
Mon. to Fri. 7.30   Mats. Thurs. 3.0   Sat. 5 and 8.15

TENNENT PRODUCTIONS LTD.
presents

THE BUCCANEER

A Musical Play by SANDY WILSON

ELIOT MAKEHAM
KENNETH WILLIAMS   SALLY BAZELY
THELMA RUBY
RONALD RADD   JOHN FAASSEN

Billie Love   Geoffrey Underwood
Jill Downs   Timothy Reynolds
Sandra Marsh   Jullia Smith

PAMELA TEARLE   BERNARD CLIFTON
and
BETTY WARREN

Directed by WILLIAM CHAPPELL
Decor by PETER SNOW

Orchestra under the direction of CHARLES ZWAR

Mr. Donkin: How do you do Madam. May I bid you welcome to The Buccaneer.
Mrs. Winterton: Oh isn't this all too quaint for words. I am adoring every minute of it.

L. to R.: John Faassen as Peter Curtis, Thelma Ruby as Mrs. Winterton, Betty Warren as Mrs. Barraclough, Eliot Makeham as Mr. Donkin, Sally Bazely as Mabel Gray and Kenneth Williams as Montgomery in a moment from Act I, Scene V.

"The Buccaneer"

at the Lyric, Hammersmith

● SANDY WILSON'S new musical play has achieved a tremendous success, rivalling that of *The Boy Friend*. It tells of the efforts of an old-fashioned boys' paper to survive the impact of modern journalism, and there are many delightful lyrics and ... The play is directed by Will... delightful décor ... well as the size ... A first rate ... the direction of

Pictures by Angus Mc...

DEC 1955

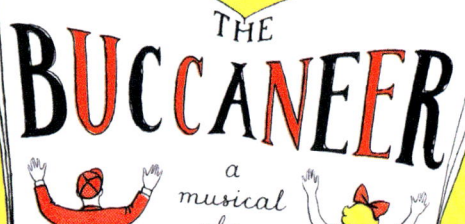

THE BUCCANEER a musical play

LEARNING FRO[M]

John Faassen (left) and Kenneth Williams (right) "The Buccaneer," the new musical play by Sa[ndy Wilson at the] Lyric, Hammersmith. Mr. Williams, one of [the] young actors, has been widely praised for his fi[ne playing of] the lighter side of the theatre

[A]POLLO THEATRE

"THE BUCCANEER"
by SANDY WILSON

Mrs. Barraclough .... BETTY WARREN
Mabel Gray .... SALLY BAZELY
Mr. Donkin .... BERNARD CLIFTON
Walter Maximus ..... RONALD RADD
Peter Curtis .... JOHN FAASSEN
First Waitress ...... BILLIE LOVE
Second Waitress ..... JULLIA SMITH
Montgomery ...... KENNETH WILLIAMS
Mrs. Winterton ...... THELMA RUBY
Marilyn .... PAMELA TEARLE

Produced by WILLIAM CHAPPELL

1955-56, cast as Montgomery, the twelve-year-old schoolboy editor, Kenneth made his musical debut with Sandy Wilson's *The Buccaneer*, based around the tale of a boys' comic newspaper.

The Arts

WINTER GARDEN THEATRE

"HOTEL PARADISO"

By Georges Feydeau and Maurice Desvallières
English translation by Peter Glenville

Boniface .... Alec Guinness
Angelica .... Martita Hunt
Marcelle .... Irene Worth
Cot .... Frank Pettingell
Maxime .... Kenneth Williams
Victoire .... Billie Whitelaw
Martin .... Douglas Byng
Anniello .... Ronald Radd
Georges .... Michael Bates
A lady .... Phyllis Montefiore
A Duke .... Douglas Stewart
Tabu .... Michael Malnick
Police Inspector Bouchard John Salew

Produced by Peter Glenville

It is a fashionable foible of criticism
› be always proclaiming this play to be
‹e beginning of something and that
lay to be the ending of something else.
Iow surprising, then, to be confronted
vith French farce of the kind that
urned up at least once a season in the
ineties and continued to make fairly

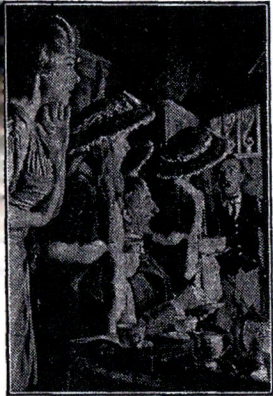

Mr. Alec Guinness and Miss Irene Worth (left) in a scene from the farce *Hotel Paradiso*, at the Winter Garden Theatre.

regular appearances for long af
how shocking to find a modern a
fairly revelling in the old stuff a:
the easy-goingness of its gaiety
neatness of its contrivances co
refreshing change.
However surprised and shocke
forward looking critics may be,
bound to admit that this antiquat
tainment is extremely good in its l
authors were writing at a time
goodness of a farce was consi
depend, not on a scattering of inc
jokes, but on the central situatic
once given existence, needed only
sion of light extravagant flicks t
funnier and funnier.
The central situation in this i
a disreputable Paris hotel wher
one of the first act's characters m
down trodden husband is offerin
tion to the dissatisfied wife of
friend. His friend has been se
sanitary authorities to investigat
noises in the haunted room sugge
defective water tank. A country
an acquaintance of both families
to find cheap accommodation f
family of daughters. A studi
whose subject is Spinoza on Pass
with the parlour maid who
interest in the subject. The r
rooms and doors are barely eq
strain of the complications that f
Mr. Alec Guinness is the q
dogged lover who is resolved to
most of the lamentable betrayal
friend, and Miss Irene Wort
squeamish yet eager lady, brings
barmaid wonderfully to life. Alr
thing happens to this pair, Mr.
even being transfixed by the gi
the shock-headed porter bores t
bedroom wall.
The crowd of daughters occup
tary inspector's bedroom and
raving out into the night, a
believer in ghosts. And the whol
culminates in a police raid whic
to have terrible consequences f
cerned. It is to be observed t
the jokes can be called "bedro
it is all light-hearted extravag
seems in the hands of this brill
of comedians to come off cap
The terrible consequences of
situation are exploited with a g
verbal ingenuity in the final act.
Martita Hunt, as a gorgon wh
melted by her awful experien
a midnight runaway horse, and
Pettingell, as the pompously
rather "sneery" husband, take
ning with enormous zest.
The whole thing is wound up satisfactorily by Mr. Douglas Byng. His stammerings have been worked through the evening almost as hard as Sheridan worked his Malapropisms; but they are turned in the end to providential use. Mr. Glenville's production is as lively as his translation is serviceable.

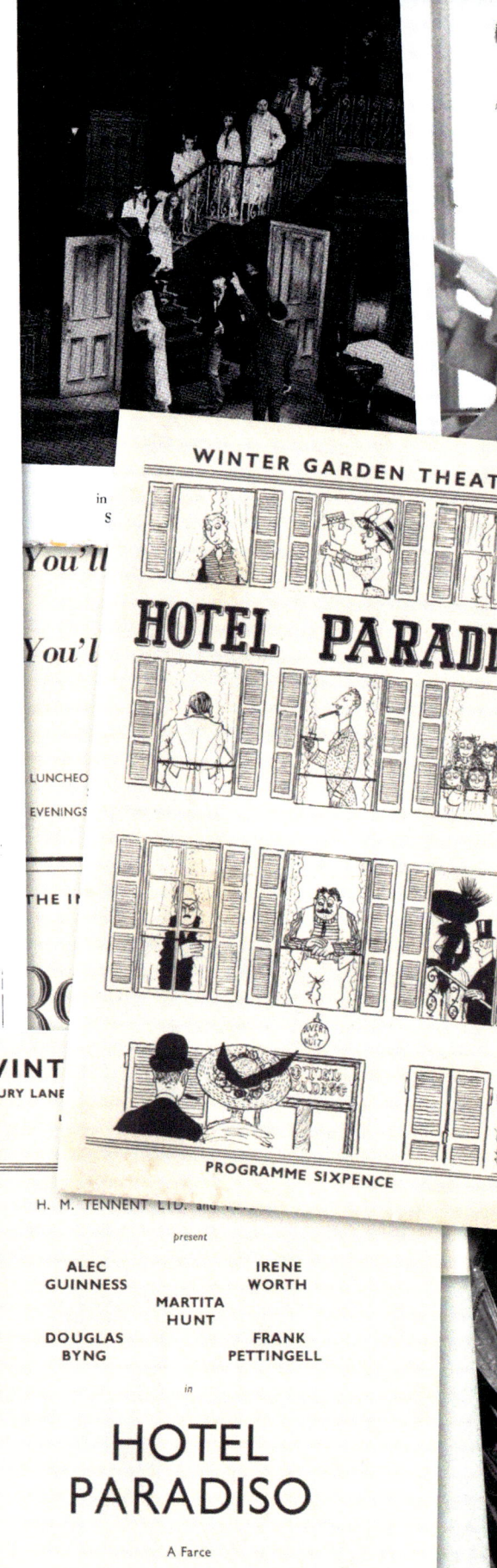

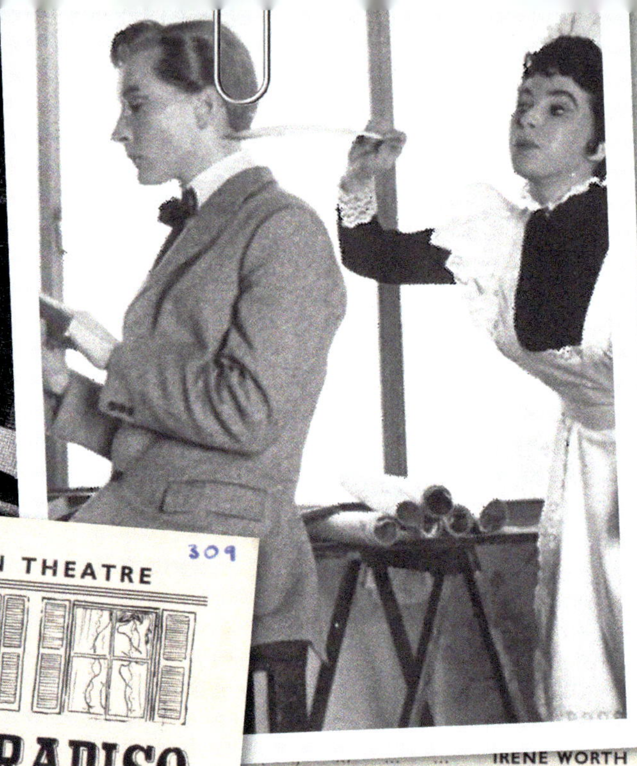

in
S
You'll
You'l
LUNCHEO
EVENINGS
THE I

	... ...	IRENE WORTH
	... ...	FRANK PETTINGELL
ephew)	... ...	KENNETH WILLIAMS
id)	... ...	BILLIE WHITELAW
ter)	... ...	DOUGLAS BYNG
	... ...	CYRIL WHEELER
	... ...	JOHN GRANT
	... ...	MICHAEL MALNICK
	... ...	LESLIE KYLE
	... ...	THOMAS ELLIOTT
	... ...	JALE DAVAZ
	... ...	ANN WARREN
	... ...	ALANNA BOYCE
	... ...	VIRGINIA HOLT
nager of Hotel Paradiso) ...	...	RONALD RADD
age at the Hotel Paradiso)	...	MICHAEL BATES
	... ...	PHYLLIS MONTEFIORE
	... ...	DOUGLAS STEWART
essor)	... ...	MICHAEL MALNICK
ector Bouchard ...	... ...	JOHN SALEW

: CYRIL WHEELER JOHN GRANT
MICHAEL MALNICK

WINT
DRURY LANE

H. M. TENNENT LTD. and

present

ALEC GUINNESS — IRENE WORTH
MARTITA HUNT
DOUGLAS BYNG — FRANK PETTINGELL

in

HOTEL PARADISO

A Farce

by

Georges Feydeau and Maurice Desvallières

English translation by Peter Glenville

First Performance : Wednesday, 2nd May, 1956

Stalls : 16/6 : 10/6 : 7/6
Dress Circle : 15/- : 10/6 : 6/6
Gallery : (unreserved) 3/-

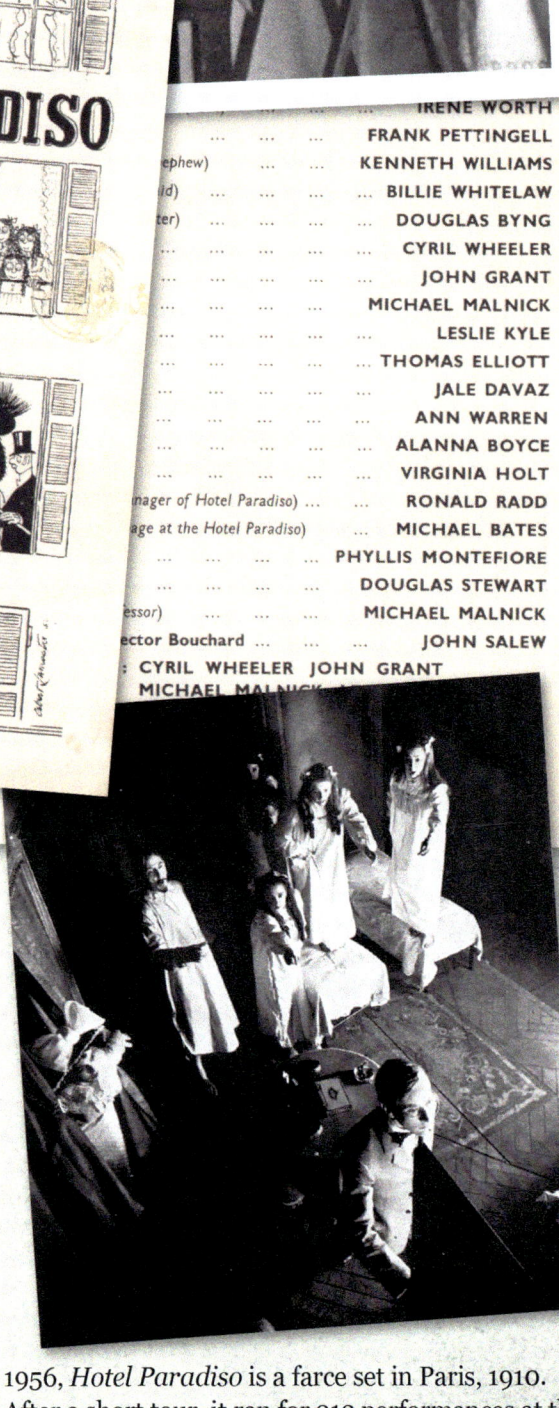

1956, *Hotel Paradiso* is a farce set in Paris, 1910. After a short tour, it ran for 213 performances at the Winter Garden Theatre with Kenneth as Maxime, a lanky, earnest youth. He is pictured here with his love interest played by Billie Whitelaw.

Spring 1957, Mervyn Peake's gothic comedy *The Wit To Woo* at The Arts Theatre Club which ran for 32 performances. Kenneth played Kite, a slithering, fawning and hypocritical servant.

THE ARTS THEATRE CLUB

Directors ... ... Campbell Williams, G. E. A. Williams

6 and 7 GREAT NEWPORT STREET, W.C.2
(near Leicester Square Tube Station)

Resident Director: PETER WOOD

THE WIT TO WOO

By MERVYN PEAKE

PROGRAMME — PRICE SIXPENCE

THE ARTS THEATRE

Administrator - - - Campbell Williams
General Manager - - - Bernard Gillman

6 & 7 GREAT NEWPORT STREET, LONDON,
Telephone: TEMple Bar 3334

No. 33 CLOSING SUNDAY, 7th April

THE WIT TO WOO

Comedy by the celebrated Artist and Author
MERVYN PEAKE

WITH
JONATHAN FIELD — COLIN GORDON
NICHOLAS MEREDITH — WENSLEY PITHEY
DEREK TANSLEY — ZENA WALKER
KENNETH WILLIAMS

by PETER WOOD — Settings by PAUL MAYO

"The Daily Herald"
"LISH BUT IT'S FUN"
...laughed at a play so much for ages
...of Colin Gordon, Kenneth Williams, Zena Walker and Ge
...tly the mood of the fantastic Mr. Peake."

"Daily Mirror"
"GIGGLE"
...for the cleverest, funniest most plausible performance goes
...the valet."

...Gordon is extremely funny as the shy man pretending to be a
...na Walker is winsomely changeable as the lady."

"The Star"
"RUM 'UN — BUT I LOVED IT."

"The Observer"
...n for the hero an enormous panache; and Peter Wood's pr

THE WIT TO WOO

by

MERVYN PEAKE

Mrs. Lurch	... ...	WINIFRED BRAEMAR
Hodgekins	*Sometimes*	NICHOLAS MEREDITH
Watkins	*Undertakers,*	JONATHAN FIELD
Parkins	*sometimes*	DEREK TANSLEY
Jenkins	*Bailiffs*	GRAHAM ROWE
Kite, Percy's manservant	...	KENNETH WILLIAMS
Percy Trellis	... ...	COLIN GORDON
Sally Devius	... ...	ZENA WALKER
Dr. Willy	... ...	GEORGE HOWE
Old Man Devius, Sally's father	...	WENSLEY PITHEY

★

The play directed by PETER WOOD

Setting by PAUL MAYO

The action passes on a summer's day in the hall of an ancient country seat.

ACT I
Noon.

ACT II
Afternoon.

ACT III
Night.

Interval music played on "Spectone" the stereophonic magnetic reproducer. Details can be obtained at the Reception Desk.

Posters designed and executed by Ian Emmerson. Scenery constructed in the Arts Theatre Workshop by Edward Gould and painted by Paul Mayo. Costumes designed by Michael Ellis and executed by C. & W. May. Binoculars by Negretti and Zambra Ltd. Stethoscope by John Bell and Croyden. Kitchen utensils by L. Cadec Ltd. Barber's mirror by Osborne, Garrett & Co. Ltd. Properties by Robinsons and Stage Properties Ltd. Armour by Robert White and Sons. Furniture by Old Times Furnishing Co. Ltd. Electrical...
by Strand Electrical and Engineering Co. Ltd....
Sound and Electrical Ltd's...
Osman's. Barrels b...
Animals Heads by E...
Photographs of this...
Kayser. Virginia Ci...

For the
General Manager
Box Office Manager
Press Representative
Stage Director
Stage Manager for th
Stage Manager
Assistant Stage Manag
Master Carpenter
Chief Electrician...

Three bells will be r
Two bells will be ru
One bell will be ru

You are requ
NOT

The Arts
ARTS THEATRE

"THE WIT TO WOO"
By MERVYN PEAKE

Mrs. Lurch	WINIFRED BRAEMAR
Hodgekins	NICHOLAS MEREDITH
Watkins	JONATHAN FIELD
Parkins	DEREK TANSLEY
Jenkins	GRAHAM ROWE
Kite	KENNETH WILLIAMS
Percy Trellis	COLIN GORDON
Sally Devius	ZENA WALKER
Dr. Willy	GEORGE HOWE
Old Man Devius	WENSLEY PITHEY

Produced by PETER WOOD

The punning title promises "a merry note": and it is struck at once by the entry of funeral mutes into the cobwebbed hall of an ancient Gothic house through whose twisted windows the owl can be heard hooting. They talk mock macabre verse very divertingly.

All too soon we notice that the undertakers' talk, for all its effectively comic twists, lacks the impress of an individual style. No matter, we say, and we settle down to enjoy the thing as a somewhat out-of-the-way farce. It is all about a tongue-tied lover who, tiring of desperate efforts to tell his love, arranges for the appearance of his own death and is ceremoniously buried. He has never known fear when wearing disguise as an amateur actor, and an artful valet assures him that the kind of lover the young lady has in mind is "a beast of genius." It is as such a creature, a painter who holds the world up to ransom at the point of his brush, that he tries to take the lady by storm, but she, taking fright, seems now to prefer the mild, tongue-tied Percy she assumes to be lying in the family vault. And so on.

The farce is embellished by some odd characters—a Smollett-like bed-ridden old gentleman who is lowered on pulleys into the hall surveying the landscape through a long telescope and flourishing a blunderbuss, a tippling old doctor with an unseemly mind and acute sciatica and the lugubrious undertakers who turn into a brisk brokers' men. But eventually it becomes clear that the author can think of no more odd characters and odd happenings. He is left to do what he can with his verse, and the piece gradually turns into a painful imitation of Mr. Christopher Fry.

While the going is good Mr. Colin Gordon is extremely funny as the shy man pretending to be a great lover and Miss Zena Walker is winsomely changeable as the lady. Mr. George Howe and Mr. Wensley Pithey are the crusted eccentrics, Mr. Nicholas Meredith leads the mutes in sergeant-major style and Mr. Kenneth Williams does what he can with the artful valet who begins as a distinct character and gradually loses importance. Manfully prepared to make the best of a farce without style, we are inflicted in the end with a fantasy marred by a bogus style.

21

-oOo- -oOo-

– NEW YEAR GREETINGS –

-oOo-

BBC VARIETY ORCHESTRA CONDUCTED BY
PAUL FENOULHET
(Leader: John Jezzard)

PRODUCER: JACQUES BROWN ANNOUNCER: DOUGLAS SMITH

SCRIPT: ERIC MERRIMAN INCIDENTAL MUSIC: EDWIN BRADEN

S.M.'S: RON BELCHIER: VERNON LAWRENCE:

KENNETH HORNE
in
"BEYOND OUR KEN" (12
with
KENNETH WILLIAMS
HUGH PADDICK
BETTY MARSDEN
BILL PERTWEE
JANET WATERS
THE HORNETS

Radio Times (Incorporating World-Radio) October 13, 1960. Vol. 149: No. 1927.

NORTH OF ENGLAND EDITION

OCTOBER 15–

BBC Radio Times
tv and SOUND

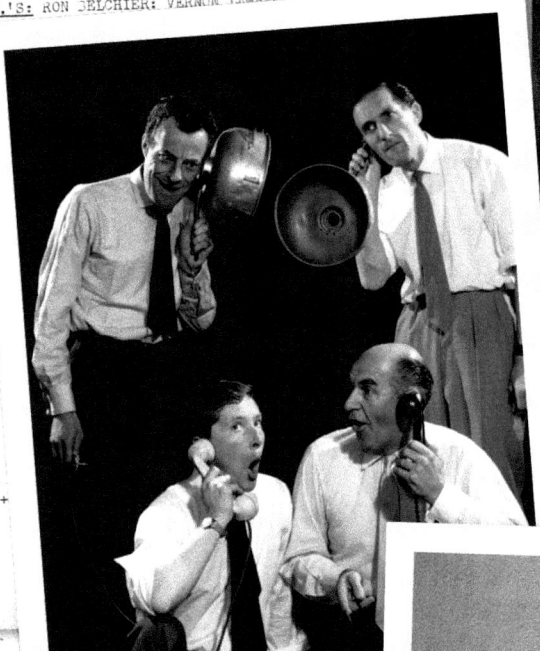

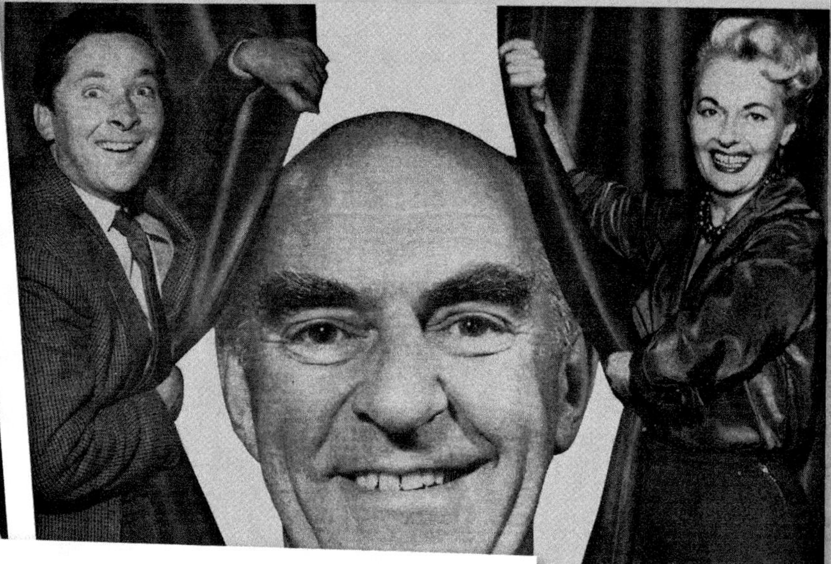

Beyond Our Ken
THURSDAY LIGHT

KENNETH HORNE
in
"BEYOND OUR KEN"
with
KENNETH WILLIAMS
HUGH PADDICK

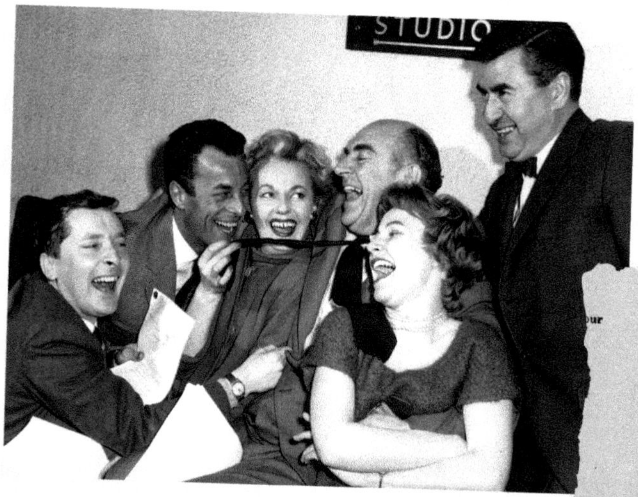

Repeated on Friday

9.0
BEYOND OUR KEN

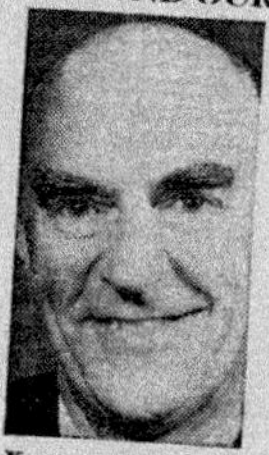

Kenneth Horne
in
A sort of radio show
with Kenneth Williams
Hugh Paddick, Betty Marsden
Bill Pertwee, Janet Waters
The Hornets
and the
BBC Variety Orchestra
Leader, John Jezard
Conductor, Paul Fenoulhet
Incidental music by Edwin Braden
Script by Eric Merriman
Produced by Jacques Brown
BBC recording
The first of a new series
Hugh Paddick is appearing in 'My Fair Lady' at the Theatre Royal, Drury Lane; Kenneth Williams in 'Pieces of Eight' at the Apollo Theatre, London
Repeated on Sunday at 6.30 p.m.

October 13, 1960

Beyond Our Ken

THURSDAY

2K + 3P + 2M + 2J + 4H = BOK

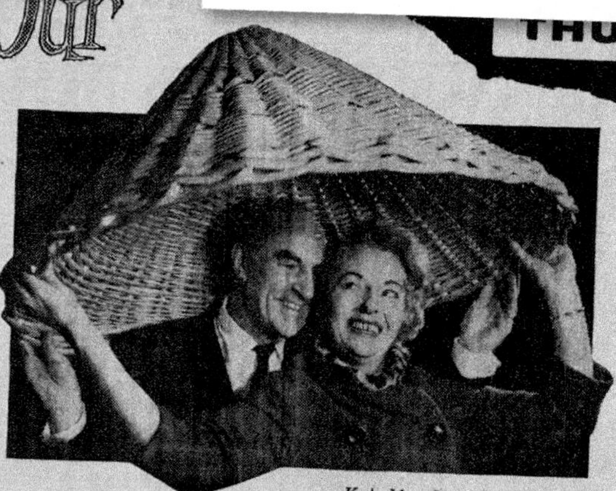

K + M = Horne and Marsden

THE cryptic-looking equation above is the secret formula for *BOK*—the most talked-about thing in radio for some years: it was handed to us by none other than **Kenneth Horne,** who from tonight will once again preside (in the Light Programme) over the process in which its various elements combine into the powerful, even explosive, mixture whose chief side-effect is laughter.

To identify the two Ks is easy: one stands for Horne himself, and the other for **Kenneth Williams** whose quick-silver properties can take shape in many forms, from querulous old Ambrose to gushy Charles. The Ps? One for **Hugh Paddick,** the substance of Snaith and the overhydrated Birkinshaw, one for **Paul Fenoulhet,** the musical matrix of the mixture, and one for **Bill Pertwee.**

Betty Marsden is undoubtedly the first M, and the other must be **Eric Merriman,** whose brooding countenance belies the verbal wit and flashing fancies that run through his scriptwriting brain. One J is **Jacques Brown,** the producer and catalyst of it all. But the second J only yields its identity to further research: it seems that **Janet Waters** is entering *BOK* for the first time. That leaves 4H. Obviously a compound element but, being the last, easily isolated—the **Hornets,** a singing group evolved out of last season's Fraser Hayes Four.

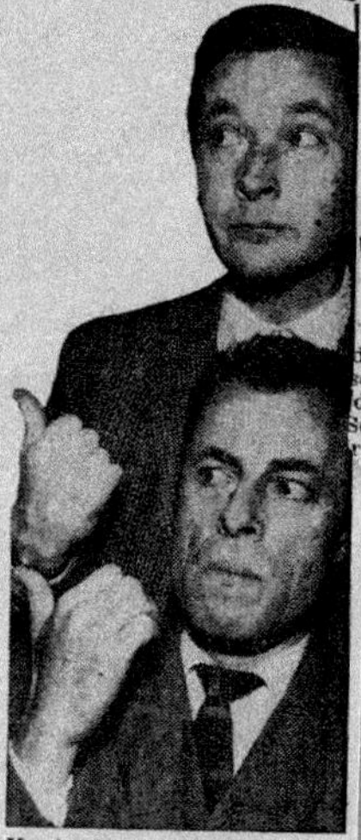

K + P = Williams and Paddick

1 July 1958, the first broadcast of the sketch-based comedy series, *Beyond Our Ken,* in which Kenneth played numerous characters and would continue to do so across all the seven series' until its last in 1964.

1958-59, Rodgers and Hammerstein's *Cinderella* at The Coliseum with Kenneth as Portia, one of the Ugly Sisters, the other was Ted Durante as Joy.

Mr. Tommy Steele as Buttons in *Cinderella*.

Taste and Splendour Enhance Cinderella Production

Portia	KENNETH WILLIAMS
Joy	TED DURANTE
Fairy Godmother	BETTY MARSDEN
Cinderella	YANA
Baby Bear	MARYON LESLIE
Buttons	TOMMY STEELE
Dandini	GODFREY JAMES
The Prince	BRUCE TRENT
The Baron	GRAHAM SQUIRE
The King	JIMMY EDWARDS
Lord Chancellor	ROBIN PALMER
The Queen	ENID LOWE
The Crystal Fairy	PRUDENCE RODNEY
Principal Male Dancer	TOM MERRIFIELD

Produced by FREDDIE CARPENTER

Cinderella at the Coliseum may be long remembered as the pantomime which Mr. Loudon Sainthill decorated so beautifully.

The music by Mr. Richard Rodgers and the lyrics by Mr. Oscar Hammerstein II have to be judged by the high standards they have set themselves in the past. The tunes and the words are uniformly pleasant, but they are not particularly exciting. Mr. Sainthill gives the impression that he has found the problem of combining splendour and taste a stimulating one. He has obviously been given all possible scope to solve the problem in his own way, and from the opening scene of the woods in winter, with the court in full cry after the stag, to the crystal caves of fairyland and to the revolving glass staircases opening on to staircases which prolongs the grandeur of Cinderella's arrival at the ball, with splendid staircases opening on to staircases yet more splendid, continually delight the eye. Splendour is nothing new in the Christmas theatre, but splendour of so much taste in design and colour is a welcome rarity.

We cannot expect fortune to come with both hands full. The spectacle seems to have a daunting effect on the funny men. Mr. Tommy Steele, Mr. Jimmy Edwards, Mr. Kenneth Williams, and Mr. Ted Durante are in some danger of being totally submerged. It is left to Miss Betty Marsden to introduce into pantomime a cynical Fairy Godmother and to carry off the innovation with delightful theatrical aplomb. When she appears in Cinderella's kitchen, a glittering apparition, she comes near to exposing the absurdity of the whole romantic fable. Whoever heard of a pumpkin turning into a coach or white mice into grey punks, and, in one of the wittiest of Mr. Hammerstein's lyrics she declares all such fancies to be flying in the face of worldly good sense. Still, the world, as she knows, is full of zanies and fools who do not believe in sensible rules and since poor Cinderella is wishing so hard she good-humouredly and casually performs the miracle she is expected to perform. But even then she remains a somewhat ironical observer of the consequences, and last night the spirit of pantomime showed its disapproval of such cynical liberties with tradition. The greys who were to have drawn the glass coach to the palace began to kick and bite each other, and wisely the royal progress was drastically curtailed.

Mr. Jimmy Edwards, as the King, has little to do until near the end of the show he is given a gorgeous setting and various cornets and trombones which bring him into a series of amusing conflicts with the orchestra. Finally he sends the conductor's score sheets flying into the stalls and himself tries with disconcerting results to impose his will on the instrumentalists. Mr. Tommy Steele, the "pop" singer hero of the teenagers, confines himself to straight acting. He is a dapper Buttons with a pleasing personality and a nice sense of timing. The Ugly Sisters are good in the traditional way, and Mr. Kenneth Williams contrives to give Portia an individual touch of comic malice. Miss Yana and Mr. Bruce Trent play the romantics gracefully; but what of enchantment the show springs comes from the scenery and costumes.

GARRICK THEATRE

share my lettuce

A DIVERSION WITH MUSIC

6D

THEATRE ROYAL BRIGHTON

SHARE MY LETTUCE

LYRIC
Box Office RIVerside
Lessees: Associated Theatre Seasons Ltd.

Wednesday, 21st August   Evenings at 8.0
6.15 & 8.30   Matinees: Thursdays at 3 p.m.

Michael Codron
in association with
Edward Kassner
presents

share my lettuce

a diversion with music

Philip Gilbert
(by permission of the J. Arthur Rank Organisation)

Maggie Smith
Roderick Cook
Barbara Evans
Kenneth Mason
Heather Linson
John Prescott
and
Kenneth Williams

designed by
Disley Jones

musical director
Anthony Bowles

written by
Bamber Gascoigne

music composed by
Keith Statham and Patrick Gowers

directed by
Eleanor Fazan

LYRIC THEATRE, HAMMERSMITH

SHARE MY LETTUCE

By BAMBER GASCOIGNE: composed by KEITH STATHAM and PATRICK GOWERS

Share My Lettuce belongs to the new genre of cranky revue, in which wit consists less of dialogue than of mime and crazy or original notion. With its cast of five men and three girls, recognizable by colour rather than name, and some simple and mobile prismatic designs cleverly lit by the designer, Mr. Disley Jones, it slickly exploits its own ingenuity of sketch and song.

On the whole it truly merits its own description as a "diversion," and if the humour sags towards the end that is because the sentimental songs tend to be altogether less effective than the comedy, most of which comes in the first half. Always there is the element of surprise and anticipation, Miss Barbara Evans (in pink) dances gracefully and the cast, though not strong in voices, hold their own in the ingenious oper...

SHARE MY LETTUCE
a diversion

BARBARA EVANS .... in VIOLET
JOHNNY GREENLAND .... in PINK
RODERICK COOK .... in YELLOW
HEATHER LINSON .... in BROWN
KENNETH MASON .... in BLUE
PHILIP GILBERT .... in ORANGE
MAGGIE SMITH .... in RED
KENNETH WILLIAMS .... in LETTUCE GREEN

ANTHONY BOWLES

GARRICK
THEATRE   CHARING CROSS ROAD, W.C.2
Lessees: PENDROLL-SCENIC STUDIOS LTD.   TELEPHONE TEMple BAR 4601
LICENSED BY THE LORD CHAMBERLAIN TO GILBERT BROWN

MONDAY to THURSDAY at 8 p.m.   FRIDAY and SATURDAY (Two Performances) at 6.0 and 8.30

BY ARRANGEMENT WITH JOHN FORBES-SEMPILL LTD.
MICHAEL CODRON
IN ASSOCIATION WITH
EDWARD KASSNER
PRESENTS

share my lettuce
A DIVERSION WITH MUSIC

WITH

Philip Gilbert
(by permission of the J. Arthur Rank Organisation)
Maggie Smith
Roderick Cook
Barbara Evans
Johnny Greenland
Kenneth Mason
Heather Linson
and
Kenneth Williams

WRITTEN BY
Bamber Gascoigne

MUSIC COMPOSED BY
Keith Statham and Patrick Gowers

DIRECTED BY
Eleanor Fazan

DESIGNED BY
Disley Jones

"A CHAMPAGNE BUBBLE

Comedy Theatre

SHARE MY LETTUCE

A **nixa** ORIGINAL CAST RECORDING
MICHAEL CODRON in association with EDWARD KASSNER p...

share my lettuce

The TATLER and Bystander, Sept. 4.

We are proud to present the ORIGINAL CAST RECORDING of the HIT show "SHARE MY LETTUCE"
Recording directed by MICHAEL BARCLAY on nixa 12" LP NPL 18011
"Share my Lettuce" sheet music published by Edward Kassner Music Company
DISTRIBUTED BY PYE GROUP RECORDS (SALES) LTD, 66 HAYMARKET, LONDON, S.W.1

SHARE MY LETTUCE

PART ONE
1.
2. Inner Circle
3. Tug-of-War
4. Party Games
5. Voices of Evening
6. Accelerando
7. Trapped
8. Love's Cocktail
9. In Which Kenneth Sings
10. The Nutmeg Tree
11. Iceberg
12.
13. One More River
14. One Train He'll Come
15. Hold This
16. Behind Bars
17. Bubble Man

INTERVAL

PART TWO
1. Spherical Round
2. Excuse Me
3. Harriet
4. Just Around the Corner
5. Michael and Susan
6. Perfect Image
7. Queer Fish
8. Lute Song
9. Menu
10. Dancing Partners
11. Clocks in Love
12. Fashionable Orange
13. Kenneth's Daydreams
14. Wallflower Waltz
15. Colour Calls

Ladies' gowns executed by Henri Clive. Men's suits by Philip Landau of Bond Street. St. Michael Knitwear, dress accessories and shirts by Marks & Spencer. Tape recorder by GRUNDIG. "Makers of the finest Tape Recorders in the world." Lyric for "Just around the corner" by Michael Frayn. Scenery painted by Alick Johnstone, built by Brunskill and Loveday. Jewellery by Hanson. Shoes by Anello and Davide. Nylon stockings by Kayser. Wardrobe care by Lux. Virginia cigarettes by Abdulla.

FORTHCOMING PRODUCTION
FOR CLUB MEMBERS AND THEIR GUESTS ONLY
CAT ON A HOT TIN ROOF
By Tennessee Williams
Directed by Peter Hall   Designed by Leslie Hurry

1957-58, *Share My Lettuce*, a diversion with music in which Kenneth shared his lettuce with a white rabbit that he kept in a box. He starred with Maggie Smith, with whom he would become fast lifelong friends.

SHARE MY LETTUCE By Bamber Gascoigne: composed by Keith Statham and Patrick Gowers.
Share My Lettuce, which moved last night from the Lyric Theatre, Hammersmith, to the Comedy Theatre, is an efficient and intelligent revue chiefly sustained by its two comedy principals, Miss Maggie Smith and Mr. Kenneth Williams.
The show admits few of the subjects usually associated with revue; although cocktail parties and underground travel find their way in, most of the sketches are based on the slenderest of ideas, which are developed with stylish assurance. It is a pity that *Cranks*, the archtype of this kind of entertainment, still exercises so strong an influence; it has led Miss Eleanor Fazan to introduce dance numbers which fall short of the general quality of her production.

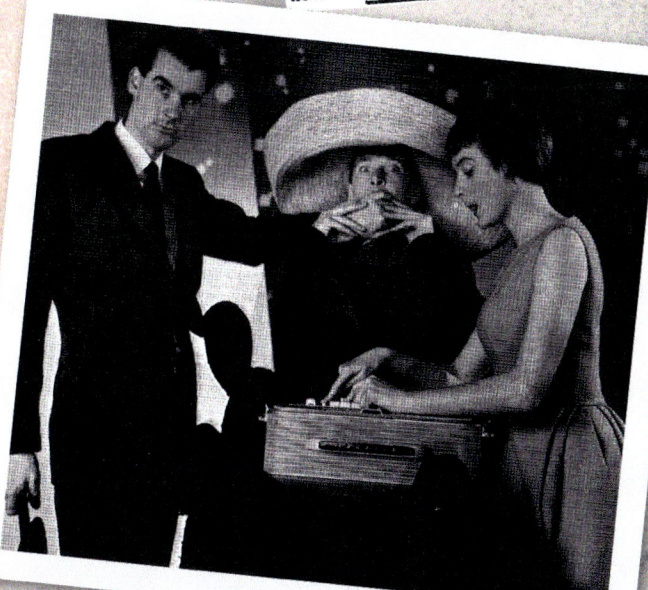

THEATRE ROYAL BRIGHTON
AUGUST, 1957
...WEEKS
...LETTUCE
With Music

Programme 6d.

25

A selection of images from Kenneth's film career in 1959. As Oliver Reckitt in bed attire for *Carry On Nurse*, the second in the series of comedy films. On the phone in *Tommy the Toreador* as Vice Consul and with Kenneth Connor and Rosalind Knight in *Carry On Teacher*, as Edwin Milton, the English teacher.

Sharing his recent successes with sister Pat. ▶

21 September 1958 – *Sunday-Night Theatre Presents: The Noble Spaniard*, live from Lime Grove Studios for BBC Television. Pages from the original opening credits book along with prints from the production with Kenneth sporting sideburns and a moustache!

THE NOBLE SPANIARD

Captain Chalford
KENNETH WILLIAMS

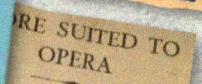

Lady Proudfoot
MARGARET RUTHERFORD

SUNDAY-NIGHT THEATRE PRESENTS

Margaret Rutherford   Maxine Audley   Robert Eddison

WITH

Kenneth Williams and Owen Holder in

'The Noble Spaniard'

BY

W. Somerset Maugham

Adapted for television by Denis Constanduros
PRODUCED BY ADRIAN BROWN

Cast in order of appearance:

Lady Proudfoot.....................MARGARET RUTHERFORD
Mr. Justice Proudfoot.............STRINGER DAVIS
Marion Nairne.......................JANE PARSONS
Lucy....................................LUCY GRIFFITHS
Mary Jane............................KENNETH WILLIAMS
Captain Chalford...................OWEN HOLDER
Count de Moret
Countess de Moret................JOAN STERNDALE BENNETT
Duke of Hermanos.................ROBERT EDDISON

DESIGNER, MALCOLM GOULDING

AT 8.0

1959-60, *Pieces of Eight*, a revue devised by Michael Codron and Paddy Stone with sketches by Peter Cook. Kenneth's main sketches, and illustrated here, were *The Last to Go*, *Not An Asp* and *I Spy* with Fenella Fielding and Peter Reeves.

PIECES OF EIGHT

A recording of tonight's show by
FENELLA FIELDING,
KENNETH WILLIAMS
and the original cast

Ⓢ SKL 4084 Ⓜ LK 4337
(12" LP record)

STEREO OR MONO RECORDS

DECCA

THEATRE ROYAL
BRIGHTON

MONDAY, 14th SEPTEMBER, 1959
FOR ONE WEEK

PIECES
OF
EIGHT

A NEW REVUE

Programme

---

1. Rev...
2. Bala...
3. True Bl...
4. In Short
5. We're going to t...
6. Entitytainment — PETER REEVES
   By Peter Cook
7. Cocktail King — THE COMPANY
   By Peter Cook
8. The Beast in Me — MYRA DE GROOT, TERENCE THEOBALD
   Lyrics by Robert Gould, Music by Dolores Claman
9. If Only — KENNETH WILLIAMS, FENELLA FIELDING
   By Peter Cook
10. High Society — JOSEPHINE BLAKE, VALERIE WALSH, PETER BRETT, TERENCE THEOBALD
    Music by Laurie Johnson
11. Getting Acquainted — KENNETH WILLIAMS, PETER BRETT
    By Harold Pinter
12. The Power of Love — MYRA DE GROOT, PETER REEVES, PETER BRETT, JOSEPHINE BLAKE, VALERIE WALSH, TERENCE THEOBALD
    Lyrics by Lenny Addelson and John Law
    Music by Edward Scott and Lance Mulcahy

---

1. Mar...
2. Specia...
3. Lost Ch...
4. Oh Broth...
5. Welcome to...
6. Cream in M...
7. Gnomes and G...
8. Request Stop

1960, Kenneth as Constable Stanley Benson in *Carry On Constable* including co-stars Leslie Phillips and Charles Hawtrey.

1961, as music student Harold Chesney in *Raising the Wind*, where he had to learn to conduct with his right hand as there were no left-handed conductors! Back in police uniform again for a cameo in the film comedy *His and Hers*, with Terry-Thomas.

1961-62, back to revue with *One Over the Eight* appearing with Sheila Hancock and Lance Percival.

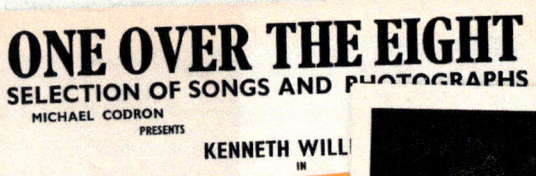

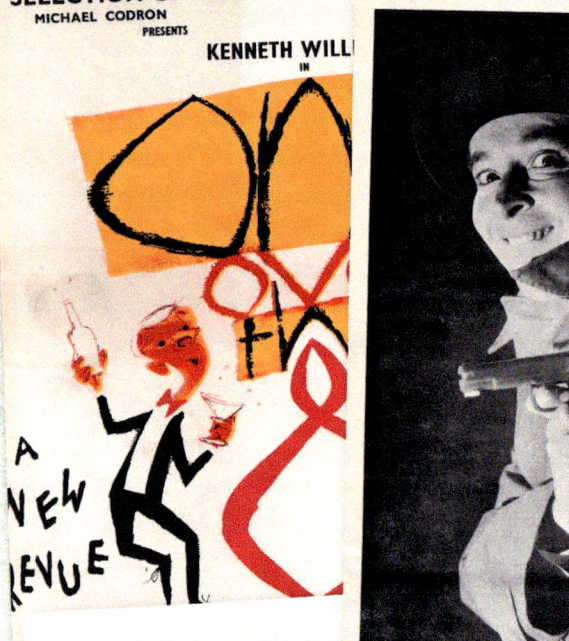

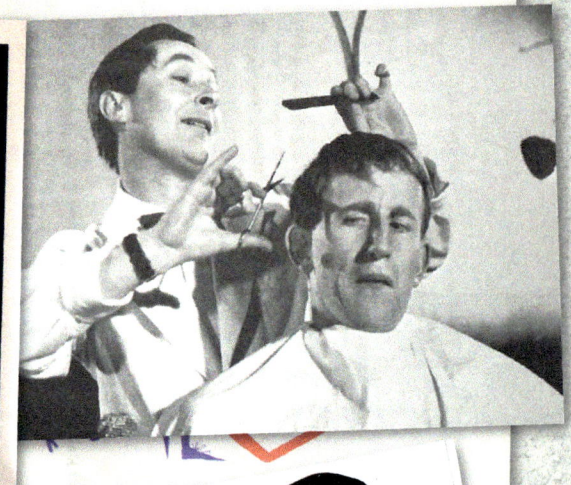

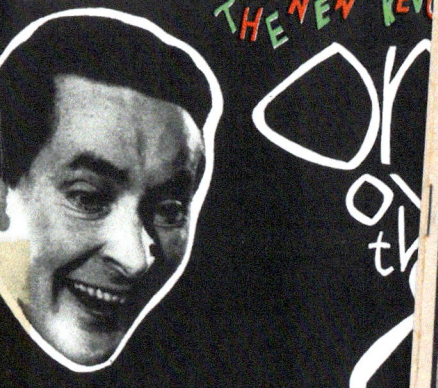

Variations On A Triangle

Evening of Skill in Entertainment

Miss Maggie Smith and Mr. Douglas Livingstone in *The Private Ear*.

deeply involved in *Five Finger Exercise*. Mr. Peter Shaffer's delicate feeling is now diluted, as if not to disturb; and without Mr. Terry Scully's strange youthful gravity to support it *The Private Ear* might seem blatantly sentimental. He is a clerk who loves music and hates his job. No doubt he marks a raid on Wesker territory, that of the underprivileged. He invites a girl, Miss Smith, charmingly inhibited and gauche, to dinner at his bleak flat. She shrinks from his records of Bach and from his flights of imagination. Later she responds to a Puccini duet and, until he is discouraged by a flattering slap in the face, to her host. That much

1962-63, Kenneth's favourite role in the theatre, as Julian Cristoforou in *The Public Eye*. Reunited with Maggie Smith, his character loves eating macaroons and yoghurt and only comes alive when he intrudes upon the company of two other people. The cast also included Richard Pearson.

33

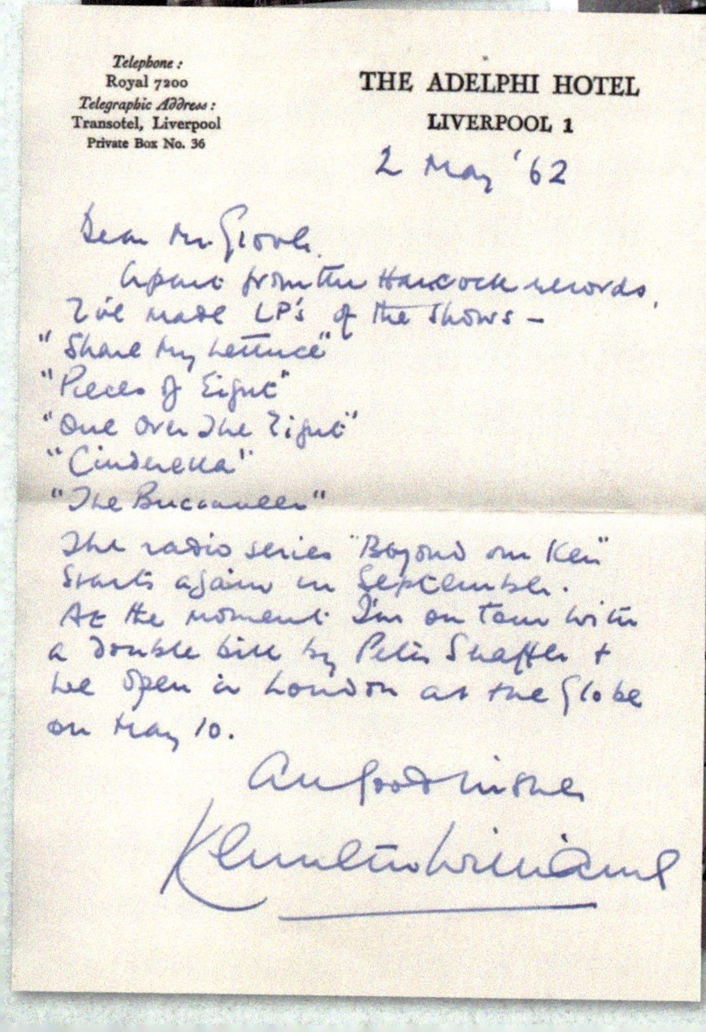

1962, *Twice Round the Daffodils*, episodic misadventures in the all-male Lenton Sanatorium for the treatment of TB, with Kenneth as Henry Halfpenny. Pictured with Lance Percival, Joan Sims (who played his sister) and with the director Gerald Thomas and Jill Ireland.

THE ADELPHI HOTEL
LIVERPOOL 1

Telephone: Royal 7200
Telegraphic Address: Transotel, Liverpool
Private Box No. 36

2 May '62

Dear Mr Gronow,

Apart from the Hancock records, I've made LP's of the shows —
"Share My Lettuce"
"Pieces of Eight"
"One Over the Eight"
"Cinderella"
"The Buccaneer"

The radio series "Beyond our Ken" starts again in September.
At the moment I'm on tour with a double bill by Peter Shaffer & we open in London at the Globe on May 10.

All good wishes
Kenneth Williams

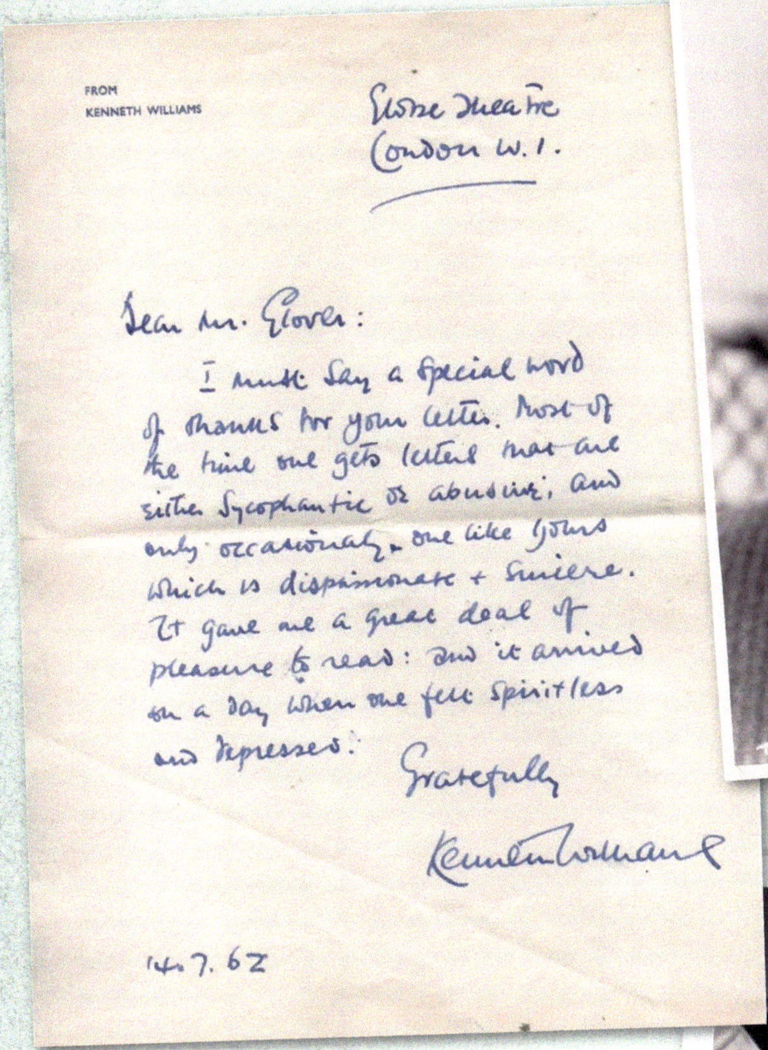

FROM
KENNETH WILLIAMS

Globe Theatre
London W.1.

Dear Mr. Glover:

I must say a special word of thanks for your letter. Most of the time one gets letters that are either sycophantic or abusive, and only occasionally, one like yours which is dispassionate + sincere. It gave me a great deal of pleasure to read: and it arrived on a day when one felt spiritless and depressed.

Gratefully
Kenneth Williams

14.7.62

1962, on the SS Happy Wanderer, Kenneth as First Officer Leonard Marjoribanks in *Carry On Cruising* helped along by the ship's doctor played by Kenneth Connor.

1963, back to the sea again as Captain Fearless in *Carry On Jack* in charge of HMS Venus with his crew including Bernard Cribbins, Charles Hawtrey, Donald Houston, Juliet Mills and Percy Herbert.

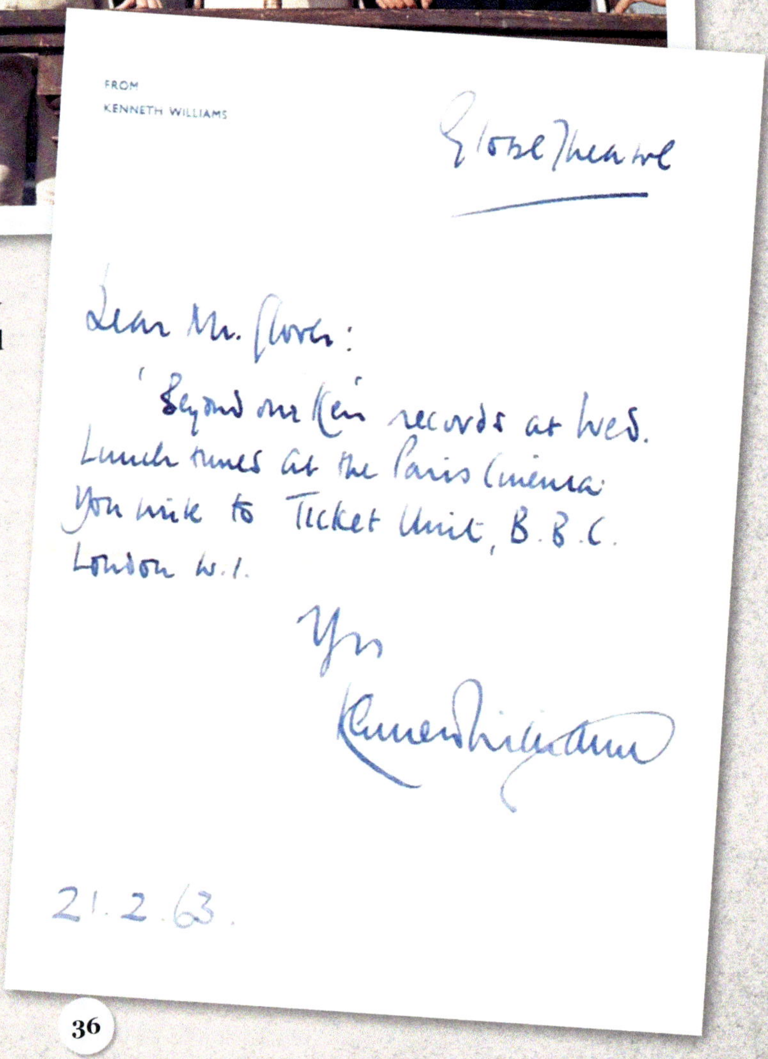

FROM
KENNETH WILLIAMS

Globe Theatre

Dear Mr. Glover:

'Beyond our Ken' records at Wed. Lunch times at the Paris Cinema: You write to Ticket Unit, B.B.C. London W.1.

Yrs
Kenneth Williams

21.2.63.

QUEEN'S THEATRE

West P & A
27th Dec 1963

GENTLE JACK
a new play by ROBERT BOLT

Theatre Royal Brighton

THURSDAY, NOVEMBER 7th FOR A SEASON OF 2½ WEEKS
Evenings (Fridays excepted) at 7.45 : Fridays at 8.15
Matinees : Thursdays and Saturdays at 2.30

H. M. TENNENT LTD. present

EDITH EVANS
KENNETH WILLIAMS
MICHAEL BRYANT
in

GENTLE JACK
A New Play by ROBERT BOLT

JOHN PHILLIPS	SIAN PHILLIPS	BARRY LINEHAN
EDITH SHARPE	NOEL HOWLETT	A. J. BROWN
WILLIAM DEXTER	GRETCHEN FRANKLIN	POLLY ADAMS
TIMOTHY WEST	DAVID CALDERISI	BERNARD KAY

Directed by NOEL WILLMAN

Decor by DESMOND HEELEY Music by CARL DAVIS Lighting by JOE DAVIS

Box Office Open Daily from 10 till 8.0. Telephone No. 28488
Seats booked in advance will not be held unless paid for within 24 hours

Seats can be reserved in Advance except in the Balcony.
The Management retain the right of refusing admission

Jacko: "Oh Mrs. Treadgold... Metaphorically... Metaphorically." Mrs. Treadgold is very distressed at the change in Jacko who has been seeking arbitrarily to solve the problems of the various unhappy couples and both she and her husband, Morgan, Violet's 'tame' philosopher try to persuade him to leave the wood and come back to the house.

Jack: "All this, all freshness, lightness, brightness, mine. And, Jacko, all true humbleness."

Jack o'Green, Pan-like god of the woodland, has been conjured up unknowingly by the Vicar and puts Jacko under his spell. In a short time the hitherto repressed and ill-adjusted Jacko becomes completely extrovert and self-assured. The amorous Penelope falls a ... changed young ...

Jack o'Green (Kenneth Wil... Bilbo, puts a sprig of rosen... desk. The play ends on a note with the murder of Morgan a...

QUEEN'S THEATRE
Shaftesbury Avenue, W.1
Licensed by the Lord Chamberlain to PRINCE LITTLER
Tel: REGent 1166-7
General Manager: FREDERICK CARTER

EVENINGS at 8.0   SATURDAYS at 5.30 and 8.30
MATINEES : THURSDAYS at 2.30

H. M. TENNENT LTD. present

EDITH EVANS
KENNETH WILLIAMS
MICHAEL BRYANT
in

GENTLE JACK
A New Play by ROBERT BOLT

JOHN PHILLIPS	EDITH SHARPE	NOEL HOWLETT
BARRY LINEHAN	A. J. BROWN	WILLIAM DEXTER
GRETCHEN FRANKLIN	POLLY ADAMS	TIMOTHY WEST
DAVID CALDERISI		BERNARD KAY

AND SIAN PHILLIPS

Directed by NOEL WILLMAN

Designed by DESMOND HEELEY   Music by CARL DAVIS   Lighting by JOE DAVIS

A. E. King and Jackson Limited, Ealing 7029

The Arts
The God Who Got Out of Hand

Queen's Theatre : Gentle Jack

Violet	EDITH EVANS	Hubert	TIMOTHY WEST
Jacko	MICHAEL BRYANT	The Rev. Treadgold	
Bilbo	WILLIAM DEXTER		NOEL HOWLETT
Morgan	JOHN PHILLIPS	Jack	KENNETH WILLIAMS
Penelope	SIAN PHILLIPS	Produced by NOEL WILLMAN

Mr. Robert Bolt's earlier plays are naturalistic pieces in which the author manifested a certain discontent with naturalism; the pressure of events edged his *dramatis personae* into states of mind which transcended naturalism. In *Gentle Jack*, he rejects naturalism completely in favour of an elaborate fantasy involving many people and a nicely balanced diversity of incident.

Unfortunately, its various constituent parts seem to be rather familiar. We have Miss Violet Lazara, a serenely egotistical empress of industry making and breaking fortunes and ruling hopeful young men through a ruthless Elizabethan charm. Her country house is in the purlieus of the woods ruled over by "Jack on the Green", the English equivalent of the god Pan, who is once a year invoked by the local vicar with politely maimed rites and unidentifiably refined symbols. When this is done, the god's temporary representative is appointed, with licence for a week to misbehave within the confines of modern politeness.

Accidents will happen, and instead of the village simpleton, the "gentle Jack" of the title—an inhibited, bullied, clumsy butt with a gift for mathematics

know, just as we know that mere instinctive life—the "happy innocence" praised by Mr. Bolt's supernatural visitant—is not enough to be completely satisfying.

At the same time, there are those whom the god of nature cannot touch. The imperial Violet is less than completely happy because she cannot have both love and complete submission but refuses to accept either without the other; but her contact with Nature leaves her unchanged, gleefully engaged in ruining her lover so that she can once again attempt to gain the impossible incompatibles.

If in the long run we are disappointed because we expect more from Mr. Bolt, it is necessary to admit that when the first of the two acts ends with an elaborate exposition gracefully completed, and the plot sprung, in every surprise; the surprise, however, is that the play follows well-trodden paths of thought.

Mr. Desmond Heeley's set is a clever fantastification, and Mr. Noel Willman's production keeps the play in attractive movement. No idea in which Mr.

Dame Edith Evans in Gentle Jack, with, from left, Mr. A. J. Brown, Mr. John Phillips, Mr. Barry Linehan, Mr. Noel Howlett and Mr. David Calderisi

LAUDABLE CHOICE OF PLAY

The doorman was certain that Pericles was an assonant rhyme for bicycles. Neither, however, should be pedestrian, and both need fully inflated Tyres.

CHRONICLES AND KINGS

The timing of last night's production on the B.B.C. Third Programme of the anonymous Elizabethan chronicle play *The Reign of King Edward III* could hardly have been bettered.

1963-64, Kenneth in the comedy *Gentle Jack* which contrasted humanity's material world with nature. As Jack, he appeared with Dame Edith Evans for 75 performances at the Queen's Theatre.

1964, *Carry On Spying* as Desmond Simpkins receiving top billing for the first time in a film as he leads the trainee agents to try and foil Dr Crow. Featuring Barbara Windsor, in her *Carry On* debut, along with Dilys Laye, Charles Hawtrey and Bernard Cribbins.

1964, Infamy, infamy, they've all got it infamy!
As Julius Caesar in *Carry On Cleo* with Sid James,
Jim Dale, Kenneth Connor and Amanda Barrie.

Is this the GREATEST LOVE STORY OF ALL TIME?

WELL...it does concern Cleopatra and Mark Antony, but this time it's a *Carry On* (the tenth)—*Carry On, Cleo*. For passion, **Amanda Barrie** and **Sid James** (who play Cleo and Mark respectively, if not respectfully) should take a bit of beating. Amanda is as cute a dish as any asp could wish to bite. **Kenneth Williams** plays Caesar, and **Kenneth Connor** is Hengist Pod, maker of square wheels. **Joan Sims**, **Charles Hawtrey**, ancient Romans, young Romans and vestal virgins head a supporting cast of scores. In colour, this send-up of historical times promises to be one of the most hysterical events of 1965 A.D.

39

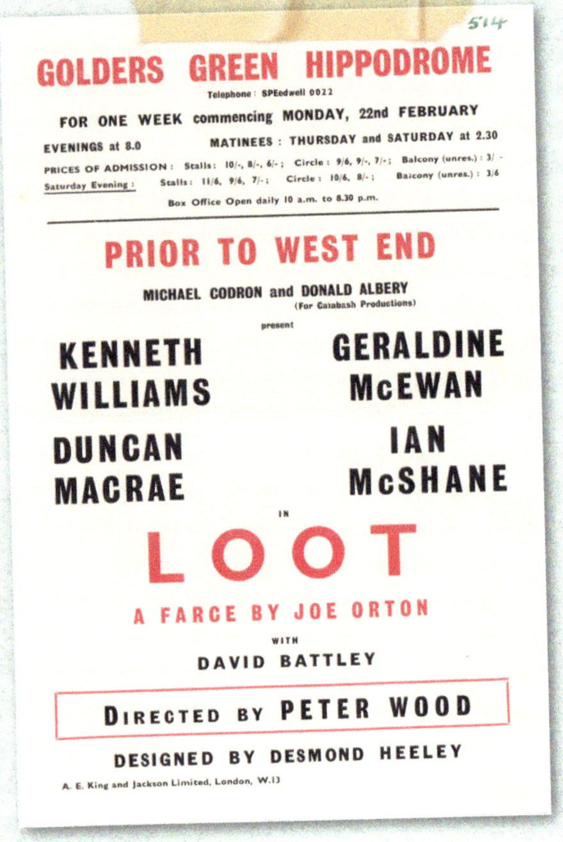

GOLDERS GREEN HIPPODROME
Telephone: SPEedwell 0022

FOR ONE WEEK commencing MONDAY, 22nd FEBRUARY
EVENINGS at 8.0   MATINEES: THURSDAY and SATURDAY at 2.30
PRICES OF ADMISSION: Stalls: 10/-, 8/-, 6/-; Circle: 9/6, 9/-, 7/-; Balcony (unres.): 3/-
Saturday Evening: Stalls: 11/6, 9/6, 7/-; Circle: 10/6, 8/-; Balcony (unres.): 3/6
Box Office Open daily 10 a.m. to 8.30 p.m.

PRIOR TO WEST END

MICHAEL CODRON and DONALD ALBERY
(For Calabash Productions)
present

KENNETH WILLIAMS   **GERALDINE McEWAN**

DUNCAN MACRAE   **IAN McSHANE**

in

LOOT

A FARCE BY JOE ORTON

with
DAVID BATTLEY

DIRECTED BY PETER WOOD

DESIGNED BY DESMOND HEELEY

A. E. King and Jackson Limited, London, W.13

1965, the black farce *Loot* was a notorious flop with the character of Truscott written especially for Kenneth by his good friend Joe Orton. However, great success with *Round the Horne* which first broadcast on 7 March 1965 and ran for four series' with Kenneth Horne, Betty Marsden, Hugh Paddick and Douglas Smith.

Kenneth Williams, who returns to the West End soon in Joe Orton's new play, *Loot*, is one of the more dangerously entertaining actors at large on the West End stage. He isn't dangerous in the anarchic, Spike Milligan sense of cocking a snook at the play he's in. He is much too professional for that. But in an older-fashioned, stagier sense of raising laughs at no one's obvious expense, Mr Williams is as skilled as any player living at spreading havoc in decorous places. All he needs to do is to talk a little down his nose and laughter follows as night the day. It's a trick, it's familiar, but it nearly always works—though there is much more to his art than that. Other players, even playgoers, can make the same noises without provoking the same laughs. The comedian's art always conceals much art.

And when you are primarily a revue comedian, trained to be funny in fits and starts instead of through the steady development of character, the art is harder to hide. So is the instinct for drawing a laugh when a laugh is not justified. Maggie Smith, another graduate from West End revue who worked with Mr Williams so effectively in *Share My Lettuce*, took some time to go really straight: to muffle her natural sense of comedy in the highest tragic places; her Desdemona was a remarkable example. Mr Williams, so far, hasn't gone that straight and most of us hope that he never will. But it shouldn't be forgotten that he spent some years in the mill of local rep, and that ten years ago he made a memorable Dauphin to Siobhan McKenna's Saint Joan. He was also a marvellously fleeting Maxime in Feydeau's *Hotel Paradiso* at the Winter Garden; though neither of these performances can be counted as much evidence of sustained dramatic acting. His reputation comes from the light musical stage; and although he has lately distinguished himself in Peter Shaffer's *Private Eye* (and may well enjoy a similar success in Mr Orton's reputedly black farce) his work has always seemed to be conceived in the spotlit tradition of revue: outrageously seizing our amused attention by every trick in the actor's book.

The chief trick is his voice or voices: a pungent middle to high camp repertoire, ranging from a raspingly genteel cockney to a high, nasal sneer of derision. It is a trick which can grow monotonous if you hear him regularly on the radio or are faithful to the *Carry On* films. But behind those popular vocal effects a serious actor seems sometimes to be lurking: an actor of oddly sinister power. Or is it just a case of a comedian taking his work with all the seriousness due to it?

ERIC SHORTER

Ionesco Talking
Interview with Carl Wildn

Pity the Puppeteer
A survey by Frank Cox

Improvisation and Jazz
Keith Johnstone on studi... page 14

Right You Are
Michael Billington interv... Robin Midgley: page 1...

Music Hall—Dead or...
Gordon Bowker investi... reviving art: page 16

● Cover picture of Maggi...

plays and players

40

1965, *Carry On Cowboy* as Judge Burke of Stodge City, which Kenneth often said during his lifetime that this was his favourite Carry On. 30 September 1964, *Festival: Catch as Catch Can* and two stills of Kenneth as Napoleon and Robert Helpmann as Fouche in this BBC production.

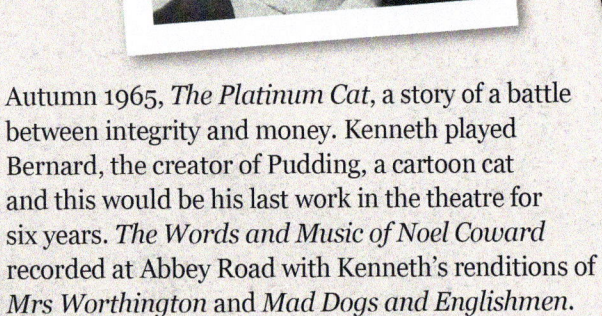

Just Ken

Cat at Wyndham's
by Jeremy Rundall

...as strip cartoonist Bernard with Jeremy
...Susan Tebbs as his temporary secretary

...directs at a terrific pace, which is precisely what he should do. Hutchinson Scott's attic set is what it sets out to be, no more, no less. It provides an agreeable, and pretty authentic, acting area.

Autumn 1965, *The Platinum Cat*, a story of a battle between integrity and money. Kenneth played Bernard, the creator of Pudding, a cartoon cat and this would be his last work in the theatre for six years. *The Words and Music of Noel Coward* recorded at Abbey Road with Kenneth's renditions of *Mrs Worthington* and *Mad Dogs and Englishmen*.

42

1966, *Carry On Screaming!* and *(Carry On…) Don't Lose Your Head*, two period comedies. Kenneth as Dr Orlando Watt and the immortal line of 'Frying tonight!' assisted by Odbodd and Odbodd Junior in *Screaming!* Then as Citizen Camembert hunting the Black Fingernail. Three images illustrate behind the scenes of the film with Joan Sims, Sid James and director Gerald Thomas.

12 July 1966, *International Cabaret*, a small screen success in the form of an all-new variety show in which three international acts from around the world performed in front of a live audience, which Kenneth compered. Kenneth is pictured with John Law, with whom he wrote the special material for the programmes.

February 1967, Kenneth the recording artiste with his first and only solo album, *On Pleasure Bent* recorded for Decca.

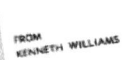

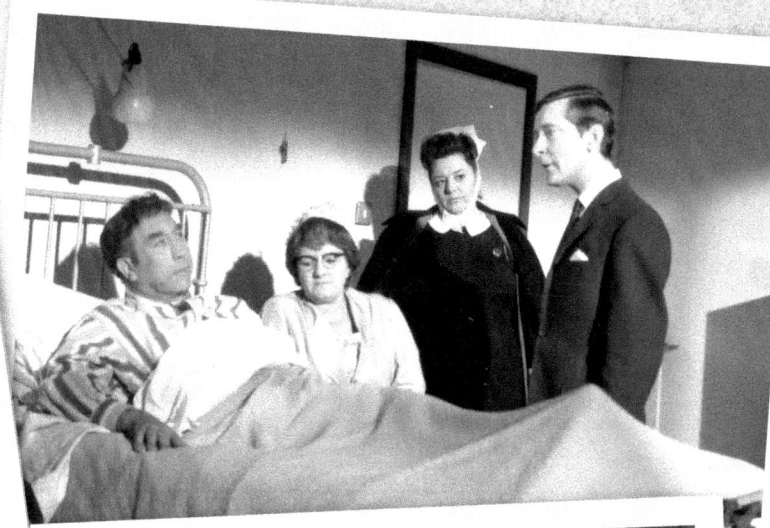

1967, (Carry On...) Follow That Camel and Carry On Doctor, with Kenneth as Commandant Burger and Dr Kenneth Tinkle, respectively.

4 August 1968, *Frost On Sunday*, Kenneth appears with Ted Ray amongst an outbreak of union problems and a technical strike at LWT. The programme went out live in a makeshift studio which can be seen here. 1966, *Kenneth Williams In Season*, four songs for Christmas issued as an EP by Decca.

1968, Kenneth on *Dee Time* with Simon Dee, in 1967 with Frankie Howerd on the set of *Carry On Doctor*, the same year in which Kenneth said that Frankie was his favourite comedian. 30 September 1968, Kenneth joined the panel game of *Just a Minute*, to talk on topics for sixty seconds, without repetition, deviation or hesitation.

A Personal Chat with KENNETH WILLIAMS

2
9.50

'My whole act is innuendo—riddled with it, ducky—but people know I'm not really like that. If they thought I was a filthy old man they wouldn't laugh. British audiences are very puritanical. They won't have any filth from their public figures or entertainers.'

Kenneth Williams speaking. Nowadays Kenneth is Mine Host on *International Cabaret* every Saturday evening; captain of a *Call My Bluff* team on Fridays; and one of the laughter-makers in the Light Programme's *Round the Horne* on Sunday afternoons. He is also a familiar face to film fans all over the world through his appearances in the *Carry On* films.

A slight, blue-eyed man who looks like a failed choir-boy forever doomed to singing bass, Kenneth talks seriously about his humour. 'People must know when I crack a joke that I'm not really like that. Sure they're in the know, about what I'm saying, but they mustn't associate me with it.

'I'm primarily a vocal comic; I've got to be. I've got absolutely no sense of body co-ordination. I look like a *stuffed* penguin.

'When we first started *International Cabaret* I told some jokes, gave a bit of patter, but they died the death. What John Law, the writer and myself do now, is personal chat. *Very* personal chat.'

Kenneth Williams invites you to join him again tonight as he adds a touch of spice to another international bill of cabaret—a bill which includes The Lavedos, Irène Berthier from France, Robbie Royal, and is headed by Gene Pitney.

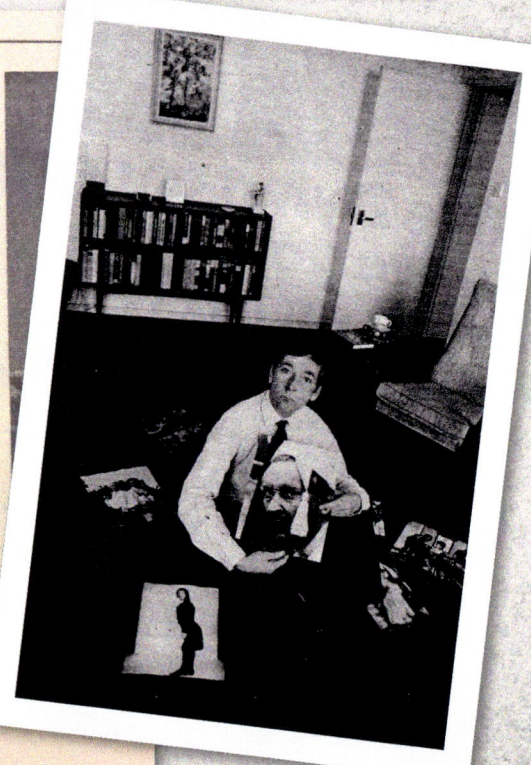

Hello, me dearios!

'THERE'S a lot of talk about cordwangling these days,' Rambling Syd Rumpo says, ' but very few people know what it really is—and those who practise it don't like to talk about it . . .

Country Meets Folk at 5.30 on Radio 1? It could be. *Round the Horne* at 1.30 on Radio 4? It certainly will be. But what really gives rise to this reference to Rambling Syd's passionate involvement in country matters is that Kenneth Williams is today picking his Million Dollar Bill for Radio 2, and Robin Boyle will persuade him to talk about *that*. Perhaps he will also recall that bosky turve where Syd first woggled his moulie . . .

— CONN

1967, with the popularity of the folksy twit character Rambling Syd Rumpo in *Round the Horne*, an evening of songs were recorded live before an invited audience at Abbey Road. Instead of an LP, two EPs and a 7" 45 were drawn from the material to 'test the water'.

1968, *Carry On Up the Khyber*, Kenneth is the native leader, the Khasi of Kalabar, along with his warriors, led by Bungdit Din, in an uprising against the British.

1969, *Carry On Camping*, as Dr Kenneth Soaper, Kenneth is the Principal of Chayste Place, a finishing school for young ladies, and ably supported by Matron, Hattie Jacques. Seen here together in moments captured from behind the scenes.

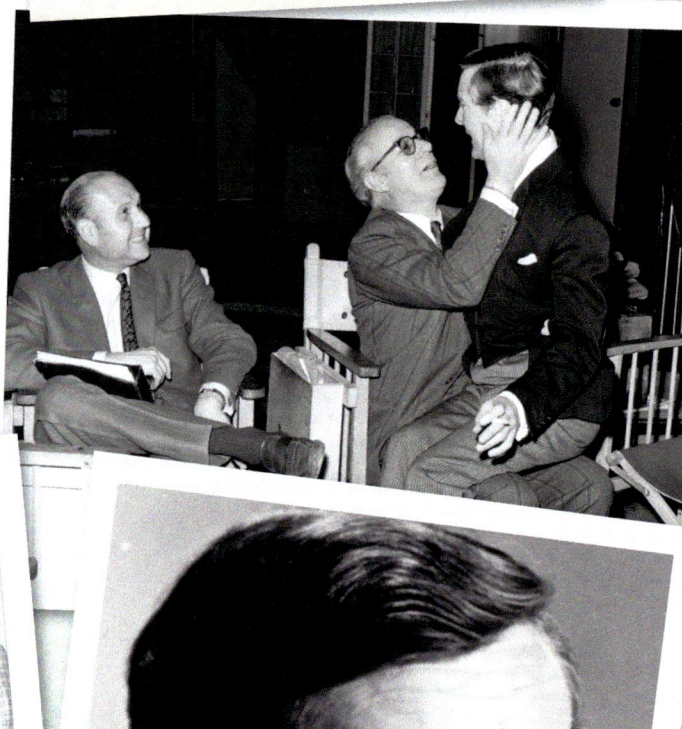

1969, Kenneth as Dr Frederick Carver in *Carry On Again Doctor*.

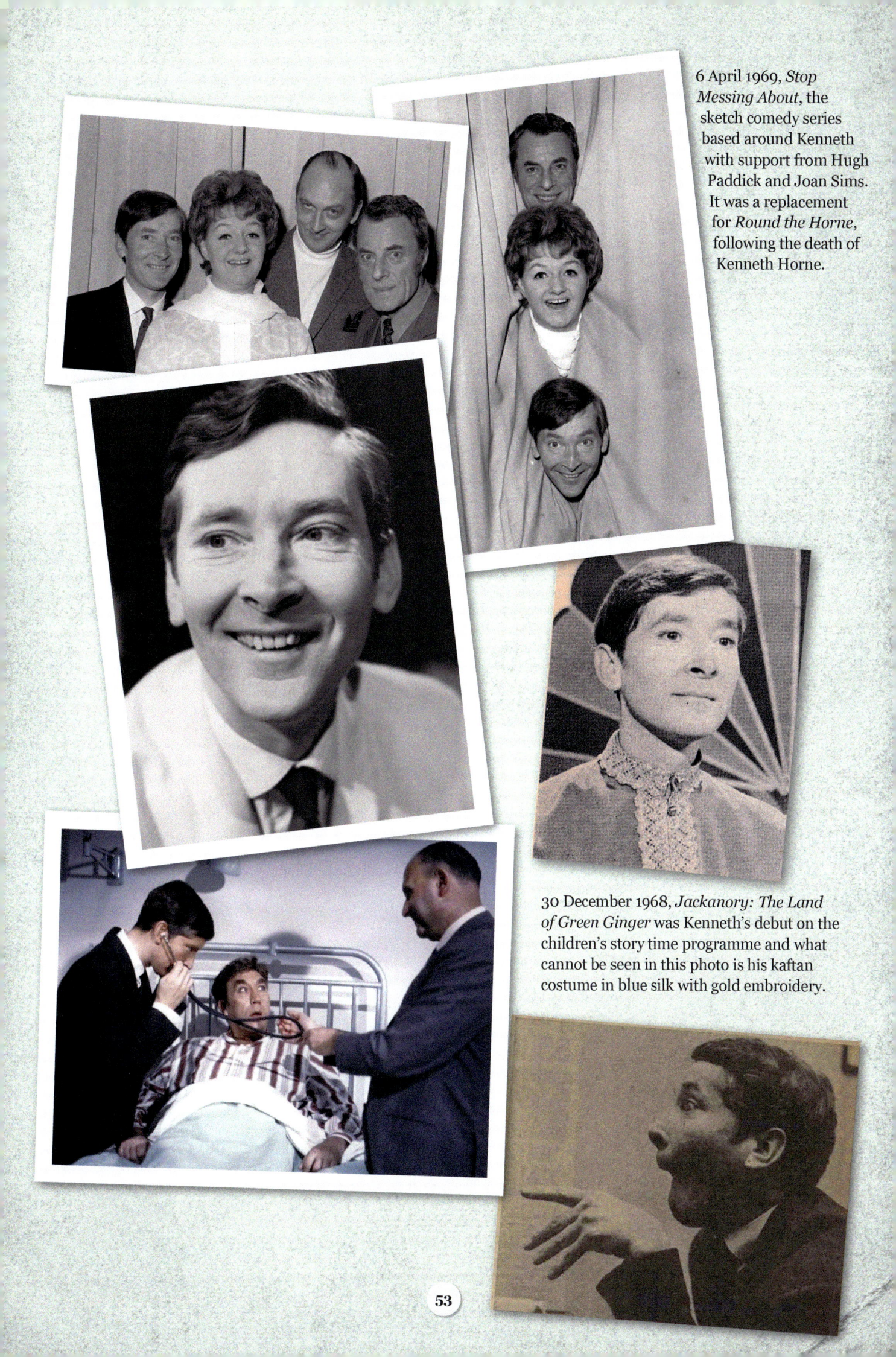

6 April 1969, *Stop Messing About*, the sketch comedy series based around Kenneth with support from Hugh Paddick and Joan Sims. It was a replacement for *Round the Horne*, following the death of Kenneth Horne.

30 December 1968, *Jackanory: The Land of Green Ginger* was Kenneth's debut on the children's story time programme and what cannot be seen in this photo is his kaftan costume in blue silk with gold embroidery.

A selection of Kenneth's holiday snaps mostly taken in Tangiers. He is featured with Michael Anderson, Stanley Baxter, Joe Orton and Kenneth Halliwell.

55

9 February 1970, *The Kenneth Williams Show*, a mixture of stand-up and sketch comedy for BBC One, with regular support from Joan Sims.

'I could teach you yer actual French' said Ken

— I was having a bit of a moan to the Producer this morning. I said "Look, why can't we have a bit more culture on this show?" I said "Just look at all those great works of literature – they were all done in verse. And they're still going strong". I said "Shakespeare's in verse, Chaucer, Dylan Thomas, Eskimo Nell". I said "We're so mundane. Let's have some warmth – some feeling – let's have some poetry. After all, who wants prose all the time. I don't get any warmth and feeling from prose". He said "You ought to try Eskimo Nell".

Anyway, he agreed. He said "Get on with it then. So I have. Mind you – it's lucky I'm good at poetry. I've been writing poetry for years – on and off – I write it on and the attendant comes and wipes it off. Anyway – I know you're all aching for a bit of real culture – so here goes..........

CUT TO COURT SCENE.

1970, *Carry On Henry*, Kenneth was back to portraying an historical character as Thomas Cromwell, supporting Sid James as King Henry VIII. 1971, as William C. Boggs, the owner of a lavatory factory in *Carry On At Your Convenience*.

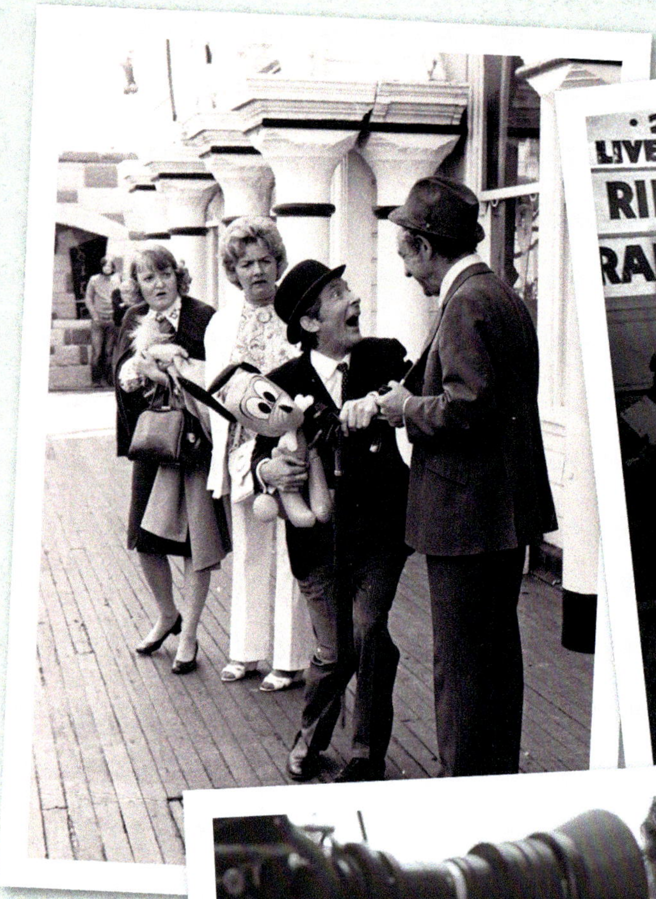

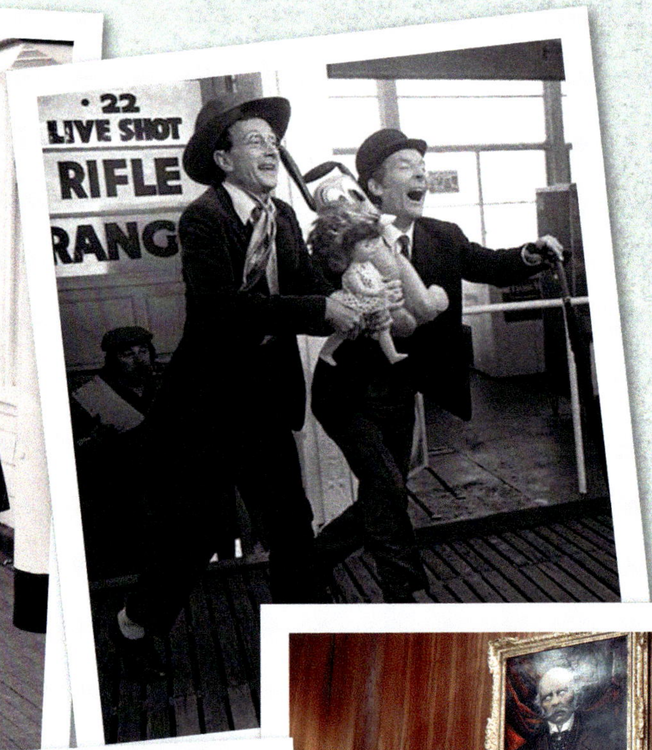
• 22
LIVE SHOT
RIFLE
RANG

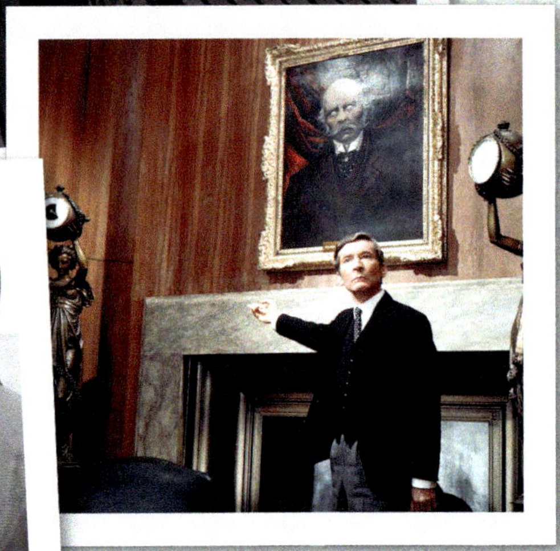

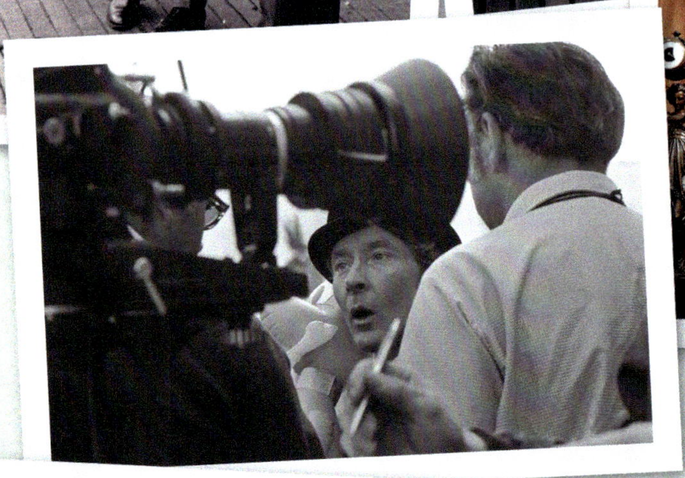

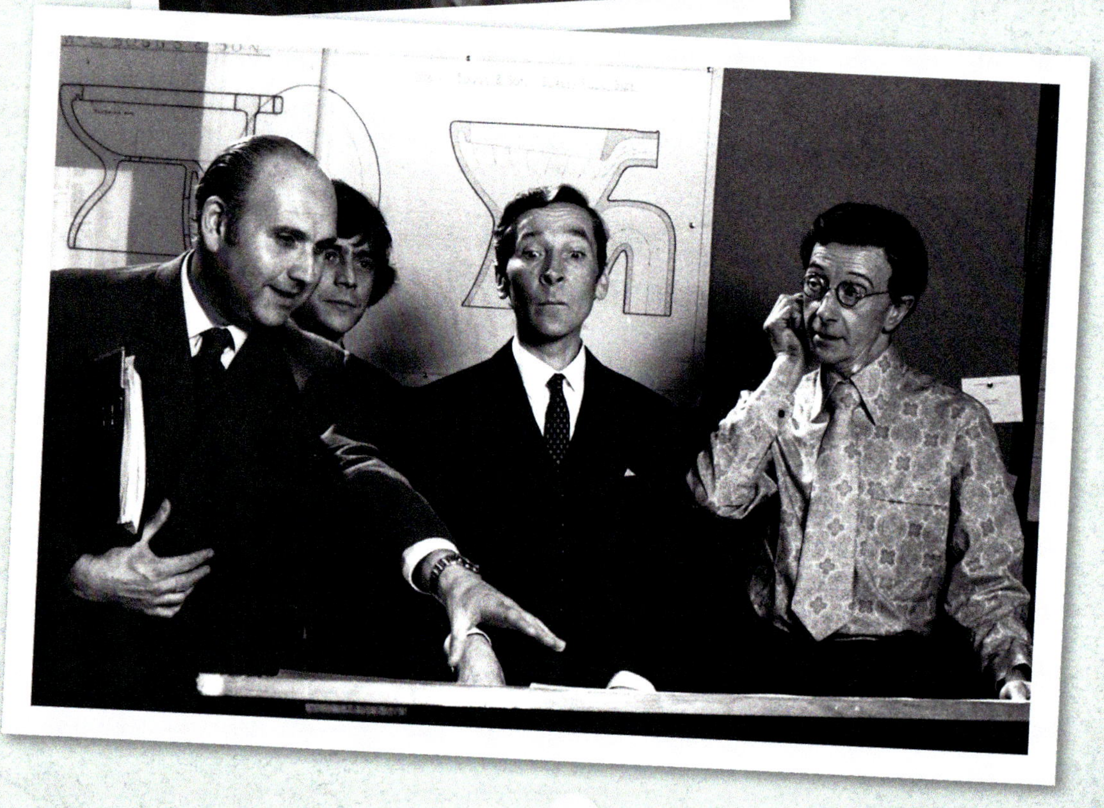

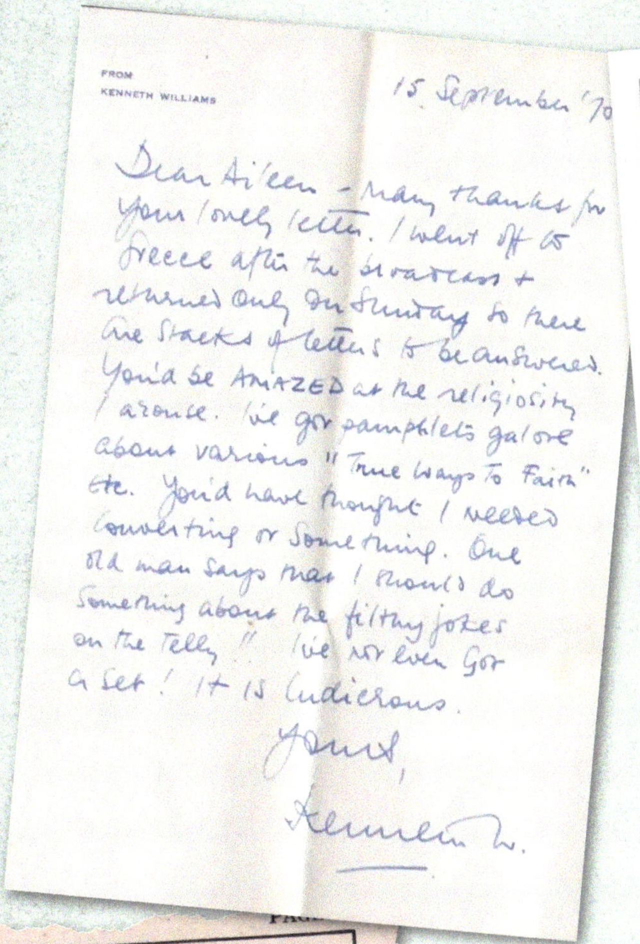

FROM KENNETH WILLIAMS

15. September '70

Dear Aileen – many thanks for your lovely letter. I went off to Greece after the Staircase & returned only on Sunday to find are stacks of letters to be answered. You'd be AMAZED at the religiosity around. I've got pamphlets galore about various "True Ways to Faith" etc. You'd have thought I needed converting or something. One old man says that I should do something about the filthy jokes on the Telly!! I've not even got a set! It is ludicrous.

Yours,
Kenneth W.

Sunday Radio

10.10 With Great Pleasure

Kenneth Williams presents his personal choice of poetry and prose and talks of the significance of his selection. Before an invited audience at the Playhouse Theatre, London

19 April 1970, *With Great Pleasure*, Kenneth presented his personal choice of favourite poetry and prose on the radio.

Spring 1971, *Captain Brassbound's Conversion* was Kenneth's return to the theatre in the character role of Felix Drinkwater, supporting Oscar winner Ingrid Bergman and Joss Ackland.

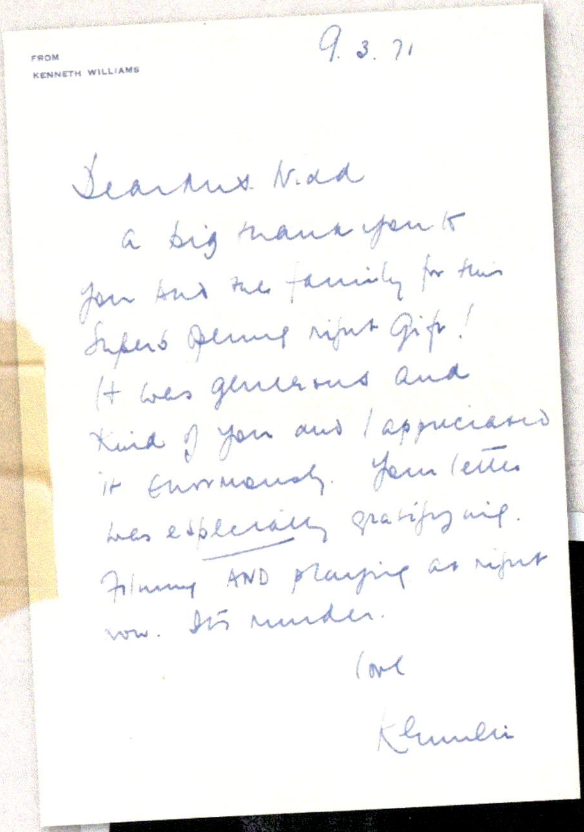

CAMBRIDGE THEATRE

UNDER THE DIRECTION OF EMILE LITTLER

CAPTAIN BRASSBOUND'S CONVERSION
By BERNARD SHAW

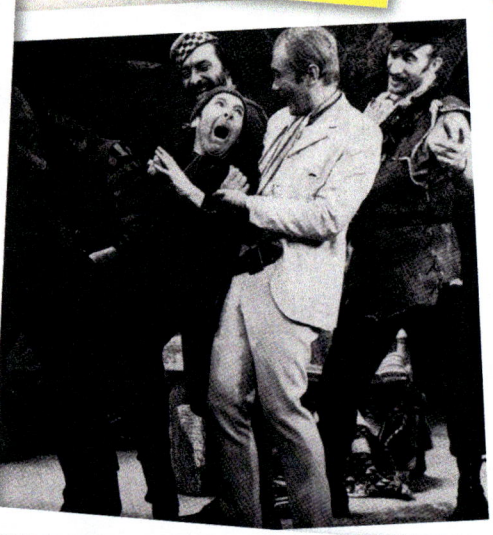

Cambridge Theatre
ERLHAM ST., WC2   836 6056
Under the direction of Emile Littler
Evenings at 8.0 p.m.   Saturdays at 5.30 and 8.30 p.m.
Matinee: Thursdays at 3.0 p.m.

H. M. TENNENT LTD. by arrangement with ARTHUR CANTOR present

INGRID BERGMAN

JOSS ACKLAND
JOHN ROBINSON   JAMES GIBSON

and

KENNETH WILLIAMS

in

CAPTAIN BRASSBOUND'S CONVERSION

by BERNARD SHAW

Directed by FRITH BANBURY

Designed by
CHAEL ANNALS

Ingrid Bergman's Costumes by
BEATRICE DAWSON

Lighting by
JOE DAVIS

PRICES OF ADMISSION:
Stalls £2.00, £1.50· ... £1.20; Upper Circle 80p, 60p, 40p

CAMBRIDGE THEATRE
at 8 p.m.
Thursday 4/3/71
U. Circle 8/- 40p
M 39
TO BE RETAINED

Thursday 4/3/71
U. Circle 8/- 40p
M 38
TO BE RETAINED

A selection of stills from the early 1970's. BBC Summer Season launch (top) in June 1971 with Kenneth More, Liza Goddard, Cyril Fletcher, Liz Gebhardt, Gyles Brandreth and Nicholas Parsons.

1972, *Carry On Matron* with Kenneth as Sir Bernard Cutting and Hattie Jacques as Matron in his 21st *Carry On* film as a hypochondriac doctor. *Carry On Abroad* as Stuart Farquhar, the holiday rep from Wundatours Ltd with assistant Gail Grainger and holidaymakers Barbara Windsor and June Whitfield.

Memories of *Carry On Abroad* with director Gerald Thomas, Gail Grainger and Barbara Windsor. With his mother, Lou, on an outing to a local park.

Behind the scenes of *Carry On Abroad*, working on *The Times* crossword with Bernard Bresslaw, larking with Joan Sims, kissing Carol Hawkins and relaxing on set.

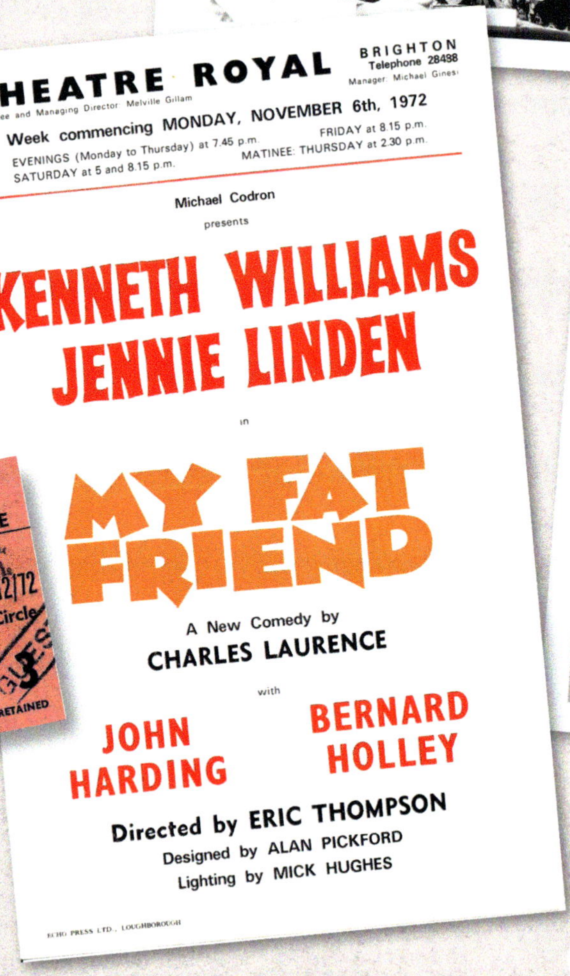

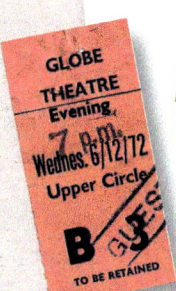

1972-73, *My Fat Friend*, Kenneth as Henry, the homosexual tax inspector lodging with Vicky, played by Jennie Linden, and James, played by John Harding.

Kenneth Williams with Vicky (Jennie Linden)—the fat friend in question

It's a grimace a minute in Vicky's flat for Mr Williams and John Harding's James

Carry On Abroad – Kenneth captured on set with producer Peter Rogers and a quiet moment on the stairs of Elsbels Palace Hotel.

2 November 1973, *Russell Harty Plus*, Kenneth was an interviewee on this popular chat show.

Summer 1973, *What's My Line?*, Kenneth joined the panel game where stars guessed the profession of invited guests and the identity of a guest celebrity. He joined Anna Quayle, William Franklyn, Isobel Barnett and Chairman, David Jacobs.

1967, release of *The Best of Rambling Syd Rumpo* LP in the UK and the Australian release entitled *What's His Name's Greatest Hits*.

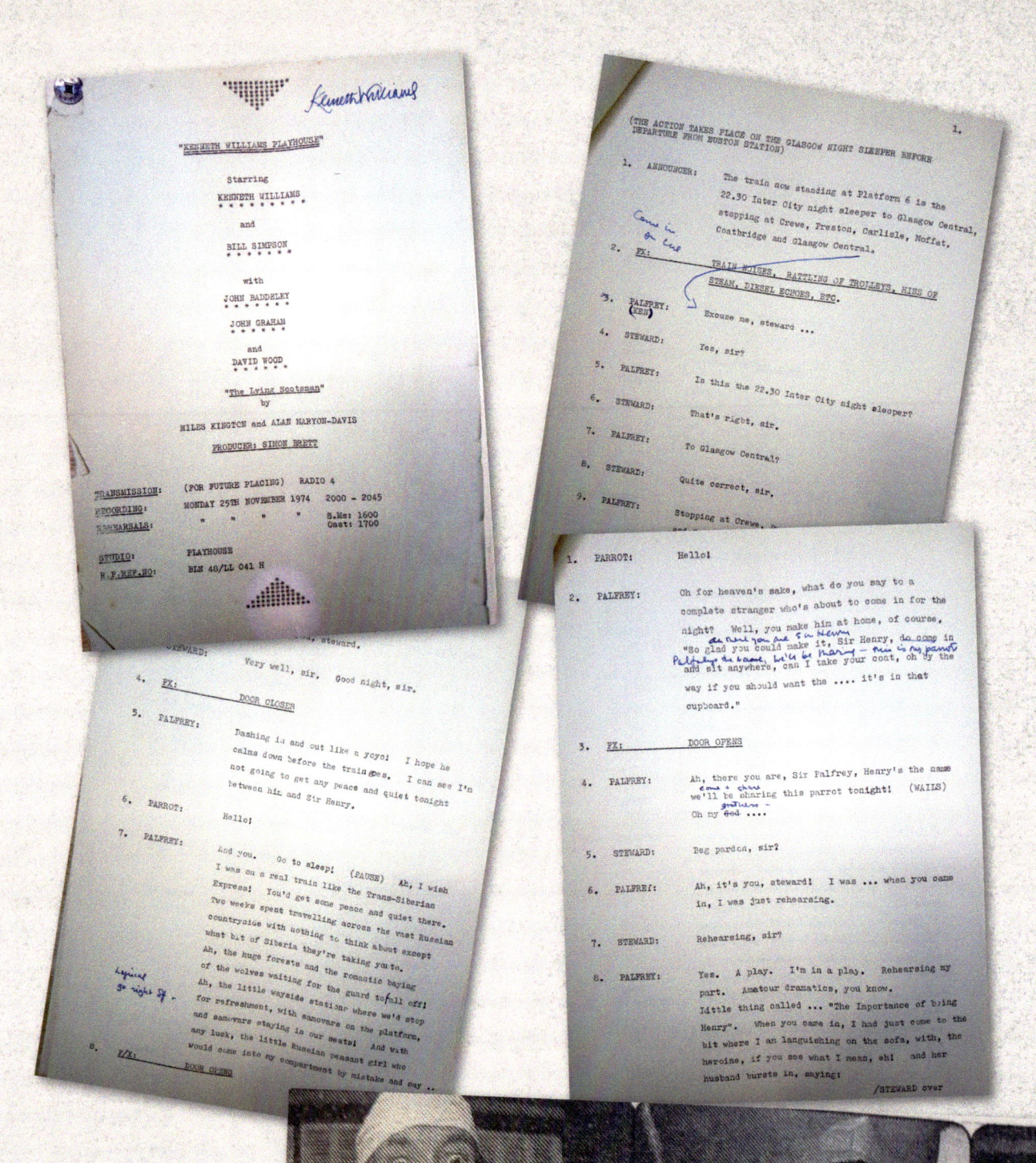

Summer 1971, the comedy episodic series for radio, *The Secret Life of Kenneth Williams* with Kenneth in various guises and pages from Kenneth's script for *The Kenneth Williams Playhouse* in 1975.

FROM
KENNETH WILLIAMS

3.1.74

Dear Aileen
Thank you so much for your good wishes — don't think I dare say Happy New Year — perhaps it should be altered to 'Happy 1975' for the country's troubles are certainly manifold. We live in parlous times. I've done a long poetry programme for BBC but they won't say when it's going out & that doth annoy me. Heigh ho!
Love
Kenneth

1974, *Carry On Dick* as Captain Desmond Fancey of the Bow Street Runners who is seeking 'Big Dick' Turpin. Broadcast in spring 1974 but recorded in autumn 1972, *The Betty Witherspoon Show* partnered Kenneth with Ted Ray in this sketch-based comedy series.

'Ooooooh! We'd never have had this trouble if we'd booked Yehudi Menuhin.' Ted Ray and Kenneth Williams in, of all things, The Betty Witherspoon Show: 1.2 pm

THE BETTY WITHERSPOON SHOW
starring
TED RAY and KENNETH WILLIAMS
with
Nigel Rees and Miriam Margolyes

MONDAY 16th OCTOBER
DOORS OPEN 12.30 PM
NO ADMITTANCE AFTER 12.40 PM

BBC RADIO
The Paris
Lower Regent Street
London S.W.1

COMPLIMENTARY TICKET NOT FOR SALE
ADMIT TWO

9.0 News
9.5
**Friday Call:
01-580 4411**
medium wave only
Carry On with Kenneth Williams
Stop messing about and ring the genius of vocal acrobatics, chief exponent of honest British vulgarity and master of risqué double-entendres.

What lurks beneath his professional clowning? What makes him laugh or sad or serious? Chairman George Scott
Call 01-580 4411 from 8.0 am

10.0 News
medium wave only

Kenneth behind the scenes of *Carry On Behind* with Elke Sommer and Gerald Thomas.

Telling stories

...anory is ten years old this week and to celebrate
40 of the best stories and poems sent in for its
...al story competition will be read during the week.
...were chosen from 15,000 by children of all ages.
...eth Williams writes, below, about being one of the
...es. And, right, Madeleine Kingsley talks to a winner
...ckanory, 4.30 pm Monday to Friday BBC1

1975, *Carry On Behind* leading the archaeology dig on a holiday caravan site as Professor Roland Crump. Kenneth takes time to complete the crossword and chats with director Gerald Thomas and co-star Kenneth Connor.

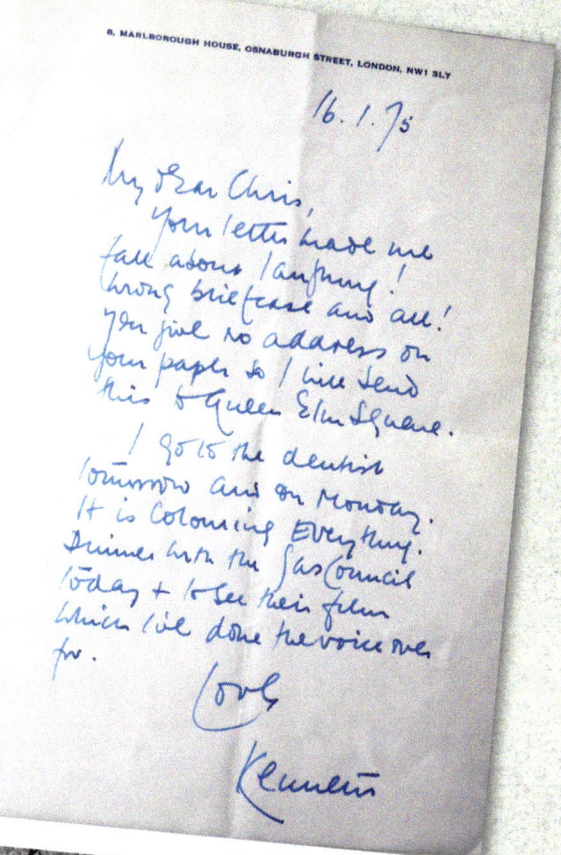

1974, return to *What's My Line?* and Nanette Newman joined the panel game.

HIPPODROME · BRISTOL

One Week Commencing MONDAY, 10th MAY, 1976

H. M. TENNENT LTD.
presents

KENNETH WILLIAMS **PEGGY MOUNT**

BRYAN PRINGLE

in

THE HUSBAND-IN-LAW

By GEORGES FEYDEAU and MAURICE DESVALLIERES
Translated and adapted by Christopher Hampton

with

PAUL HARDWICK

BARRY STANTON   PETER GLAZE
Jane Carr   Alun Lewis   Floella Benjamyn

and

GERALD JAMES

Designed by STEFANOS LAZARIDIS   Costumes designed by BEATRICE DAWSON   Lighting by DAVID HERSEY

Directed by

PATRICK GARLAND

PROGRAMME 15p

Summer 1976, after a three-year break, a return to the theatre in *The Husband-in-Law* which changed its name to *Signed and Sealed* for the West End. A farce based around a bridegroom who unwittingly marries his own mother-in-law. Kenneth as Barillon and ably supported by Peggy Mount and Floella Benjamin.

8, MARLBOROUGH HOUSE, OSNABURGH STREET, LONDON, NW1 3LY

no need to write   5.10.76

Dear Tom,

My unspeakable thanks to you for your kindness today. I never DREAMED that sitting for a painter would be QR easy & relaxing as that! I think it's incredible that you can work so concentratedly & speedily, converse with someone, and then end a portrait so brilliantly. It was kind of you to give me the book. I shall treasure that.

Sincerely yours,
Kenneth

21 January 1976, one-off comedy special *The Kenneth Williams Show* for BBC Two with Lance Percival who was also in the radio series *Oh, Get On With It!* Broadcast in early 1976, the sketch-based comedy series also included Miriam Margolyes. Released in November 1976, *The Bona Album of Julian and Sandy* reunited Kenneth with Hugh Paddick and Barry Took took on the role of Kenneth Horne.

6.15 Oh, Get On With It!
starring Kenneth Williams with Lance Percival Miriam Margolyes and the Nic Rowley Trio
Script by PETER SPENCE with additional material by COLIN BOSTOCK-SMITH, JEREMY BROWNE, TOM MAGEE-ENGLEFIELD and DAVID RENWICK
Producer SIMON BRETT
(Repeated: Friday 12.27 pm)

6.45 The Archers
(Repeated: Thursday 1.30 pm)

THE APPLICANT

(David Nobbs & Peter Vincent)

AN OFFICE AT THE BBC. A BBC PERSONNEL OFFICER SITS BEHIND A DESK. ON THE DESK ARE SOME PAPERS AND A HANDSOME POT PLANT. HIS SECRETARY ENTERS.

SEC:
Mr. Rankin is here, sir, the gentleman who wrote applying for a job as a sports commentator.

PERSONNEL OFF:
Oh well, I suppose I'd better see him. Send him in.

SEC:
Come in, Mr. Rankin.

KENNETH ENTERS. AS HE CROSSES THE ROOM AND SITS DOWN HE TALKS FAST AND EXCITEDLY IN THE STYLE OF A SPORTS COMMENTATOR.

KENNETH:
I'm walking into the room now to apply for a job as sports commentator, I'm walking across the room, I'm almost at the chair, I'm there, I'm sitting down – and I have sat down.

The BONA ALBUM of Julian & Sandy

Starring KENNETH WILLIAMS HUGH PADDICK and BARRY TOOK

22 May 1977, *A Night of a Hundred Stars* in aid of the Queen's Silver Jubilee Appeal. Kenneth recited Shakespeare and had a solo spot, though his part was edited out of the broadcast version. 1977, *Fandango* – animated adventures, narrated by Kenneth, presenting many Christian principles. 1982, Kenneth read Richmal Crompton's *William Stories* for EMI and as a regular on *Just a Minute* with its Chairman Nicholas Parsons.

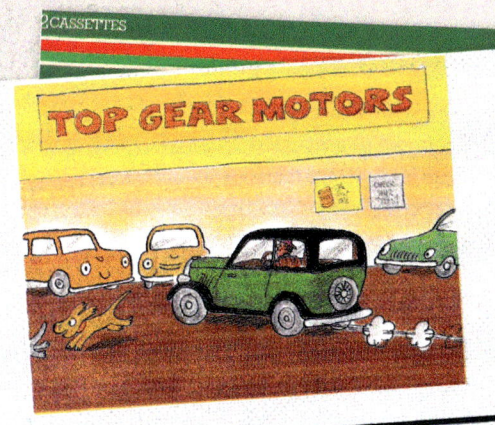

Five adventures of an ageing car and his friends

Narrated by Kenneth Williams

5.5
Let's Make a Musical
starring Roy Castle
with Toni Arthur
Joe Brown, Lance Percival
Kenneth Williams, David Wood
accompanied by JOHNNY PEARSON
and GEOFF SANDERS at the two pianos.
In this programme ROY and the team tell the story and sing some of the songs from the musical *Pickwick*.
Based on Dickens's famous character of that name, it includes such hit numbers as 'If I Ruled the World'.
Musical director JOHNNY PEARSON
Choreographer SALLY GILPIN
Designer KEN STARKEY
Producer ALAN RUSSELL

5.35 Captain Pugwash
Flood Tide (*Repeat*)

12.27 *New series*
Quote . . . Unquote
The highly acclaimed quotation game in which Kenneth Williams, Alan Coren, Richard Ingrams and Norma Shepherd are quizzed on sayings famous, funny and fatuous.
'To me, Thursday evening has always been pink, with a faint green stripe growing broader towards 9 o'clock...

REVIEW

Kenneth Williams asks, 'Is Pantomime declining?'

Nothing like a Dame

THE beginnings of drama take us to Athens, but for the origins of pantomime, all roads undoubtedly lead to Rome, and a pretty disgusting Rome at that. Suetonius tells us that during the reign of Caligula there was staged 'a pantomime called *Laureolus* in which the leading character had to die while escaping and vomit blood'. This was followed by a 'humorous epilogue'. Strong stomachs they must have had.

In fact, it all began long before that, as Dr F. R. Cowell reminds us in *The Birth of Western Civilisation*: 'When Greek comedies came to Rome in the second century BC, in the translations of Plautus and Terence, they were very popular. As entertainment for the masses, however, they did not survive, but were replaced by slapstick pantomime and worse.' In *The Frank Muir Book* we find: 'The fifth-century historian Zosimus blamed...

The form changed as the years went on, according to the dictates of fashion, but the essential ingredients remained the same: the separated lovers who eventually unite, the clowns who provide the fun, and the element of magic. Harlequin can become invisible, lamps can produce a genie, wands wreak transformations, beans grow stalks reaching the land of giants.

Taking *commedia dell'arte* as the starting-point, Omnibus presented **The Story of Pantomime**, an investigation into the origins of this peculiarly hybrid entertainment. Because so much of the traditional 'panto' was comical invention 'business' and so on, the record of what actually happened is scanty indeed, and this represented a problem for the Omnibus team. They got over it by finding all the early drawings of the various scenes with the captions written underneath. Then they filmed a team of actors interpreting these drawings, ad libbing a modern equivalent of the scene, and converting 17th-century evidence into amusing lines and situations readily understood by 20th-century children.

A versatile cast put through its paces by an inventive director

We saw a versatile cast being put through their paces by an inventive director who admitted: 'We got all this from the pictures'; and they recaptured the mime and buffoonery of Pantaloon's ludicrous wooing of Columbine much as it must have been performed over 200...

ing moment on stage, followed by the shot of a child reacting. We saw the young eyes, wide with apprehension and wonder. When they called out to the actors, they got replies; sitting at home watching their screens, their calls would have gone unnoticed. Only in the theatre can this reciprocity become so vocal and so fruitful. When a huge tomato lumbered on stage, you heard a small boy asking: 'What's that? A vegetable!'; and he quickly informed Harlequin: 'He went that way!' His concern was singularly moving; you knew that, involuntarily, he wanted to help.

The Brokers' Men — the modern equivalent of Clown and Pantaloon

The programme traced the various influences on pantomime from clowns like Grimaldi, via principal boys like Harriet Vernon, to Dan Leno as Dame in 1902, illustrating the rise of a new kind of comic — the female impersonator. We saw shots of Norman Evans and Clarkson Rose, and were shown the intricacies of the Jewel and Warriss 'Haunted Bedroom' set.

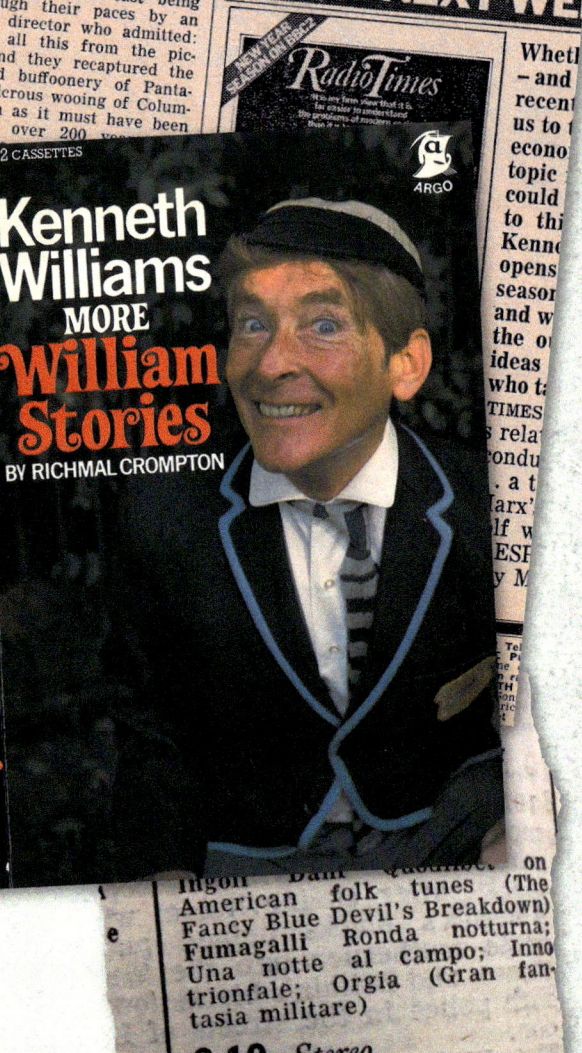

1977, Kenneth became a regular panelist for the radio quiz *Quote... Unquote* and from 1975 wrote a number of 'Previews' for the *Radio Times*. *More William Stories* followed in 1983.

80

FROM
KENNETH WILLIAMS

5.12.78

Moncher Ray,

Louie enjoys it all! Whiskey, gin, brandy. You name it! Very sweet of you to think of her. I'm rushing off to Lime Grove for this Jackanory Children's Competition. Five days & doing all in!

love
Kennie

1978, Kenneth's last *Carry On* film and his 26th in the series, *Carry On Emmanuelle* as the French Ambassador, Emile Prevert (utilising a French accent) married to Emmannuelle, played by Suzanne Danielle.

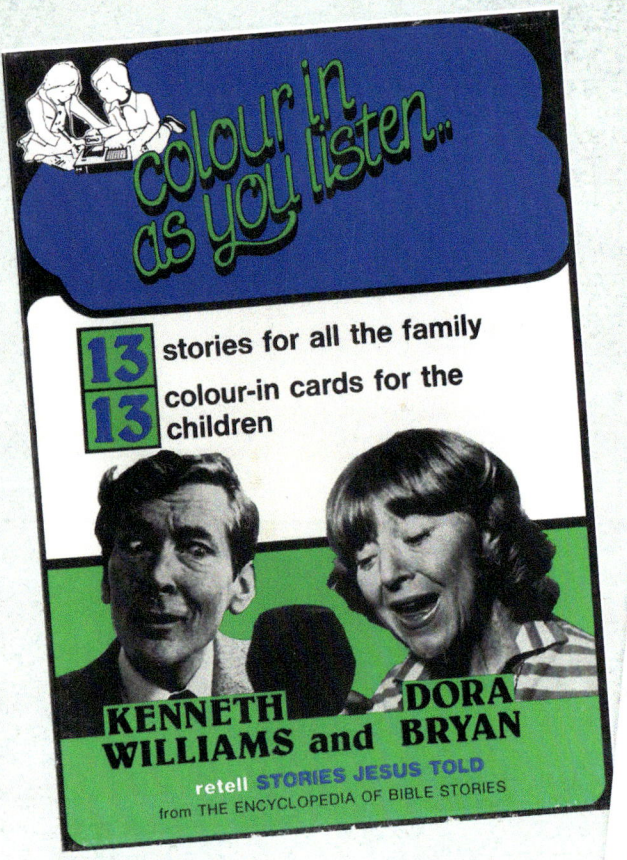

colour in as you listen...

13 stories for all the family
13 colour-in cards for the children

KENNETH WILLIAMS and DORA BRYAN
retell **STORIES JESUS TOLD**
from THE ENCYCLOPEDIA OF BIBLE STORIES

1977, *Kenneth Williams and Dora Bryan Retell Stories Jesus Told* for the Encyclopedia of Bible Stories. 1979, the release of the audio version of *The Wind in the Willows* by EMI. Whilst on the small screen in 1978, *Tell Me Another*, *The Electric Theatre Show* and *Jackanory: The Dribblesome Teapots*.

Kenneth Williams provides a shocking moment while being medically examined in Carry On Emmannuelle.

KENNETH WILLIAMS says CARRY ON SHOCKING

THE VETERAN OF THE CARRY ONs IS INTERVIEWED BY CATHERINE O'BRIEN

How did you come to meet producer Peter Rogers and perform in the very first of the thirty Carry On films?
Peter Rogers and director Gerald Thomas came to see a successful revue I was in at the time called "Share My Lettuce". They were casting Carry On Sergeant without any idea that it was going to be the first of a record-breaking series. They thought I would be ideal for the toffee-nosed recruit, the kind that keeps saying things like "I don't really want to wear this kind of uniform" to the officer. He knew a lot about slapstick comedy. He was desperately anxious to form a nucleus of a team here, and when he interviewed me with this in mind, his voice and character absolutely imbued me. I went out talking exactly like him, and I used the character for this mad old western judge.

What has been your favourite role in the series?
The judge in Carry On Cowboy. I based that on an interview I had with American producer Hal Roach who was over here hoping to persuade me to Carry On making interesting films. He was a personality who not only teamed with Hardy, but who also made some great Laurel and Hardy comedies, with Will Rogers. Another of my favourite roles has been the latest – Emile Prevert, a foreign diplomat at the Court of St. James whose sexy, naughty wife threatens to topple the Government. The film is not to be outraged than bored. They say I'm demonic in humour in the sense that I think people need somebody to wake up their mental processes.

People need to be peppered or even outraged occasionally. Our national comedy and drama is packed with earthy familiarity and honest vulgarity. Clean vulgarity can be very shocking, and that, in my view, gives a greater involvement.

The Carry Ons are vulgar but innocent. Adults in the audience can see themselves or someone been totally dull. Surely it's more seems to ask all the questions that have ever been asked about life. Certainly I went through that phase. But in the thirty years I've been asking I've learned that my forte is comedy. And I think that what you can do reasonably well is what you should stick to in the main.

But would you be interested if someone offered you something totally different?
Yes, but I'd like it to represent both sides of the coin. It's important to remember that, as far as drama is concerned, there is one coin. On the one side you've got a laughing face, and on the other a doleful face, but they are the same coin and as long as we have that quality in a performance, then I think an audience is going to get their money's worth. They're not if you only present one side, like the heavy drama side – unrelieved tragedy, frustration and so on.

Has anyone had a decisive influence on your career?
There's one man who influenced my approach to comedy from the beginning, but he's not a man many people know much about. He was John Vere who played the bishop in "Hancock's Half Hour". His mainspring for getting laughs was a built-in sense of indignation. That quality is also inherent in some of Edith Evans's best work. I quickly got on to this in comedy. In Carry On Sergeant there was a fundamental indignation about being subjected to almost everything in the army.

If you hadn't been an actor, what other profession would you have enjoyed?
Originally I was a draughtsman, simply because my school reports said "his only aptitude is for drawing." But being in the army and meeting the people I did meet gave me the courage to throw it all overboard and risk unemployment to do the kind of work I loved. But if I had to choose now what profession I would go into, I would certainly plump for teaching because I like children and get on well with them. I would teach literature and drama for then I would be able to enjoy the great poetry in the corpus of English literature. To get into that field in England you need an enormous number of qualifications – except of course through the medium of children's television, which I already do to a degree like "Jackanory".

Were you interested in making people laugh in your career before acting?
Yes, I was interested in it from school but not professionally. The compulsion came because I met people like Stanley Baxter in the Army Concert Unit and got fired by the idea of being liked by such people. What a lovely thing, I thought, to have a career alongside them

---

KENNETH GRAHAME
THE WIND IN THE WILLOWS
READ BY **KENNETH WILLIAMS**

PLAYING TIME APPROX 2 HOURS

82

1978, the release of *Parlour Poetry* with Kenneth reciting prose and verse from the Victorian age. 15 October 1978, stills from *Star Turn Challenge* as part of the Carry On team with Kenneth Connor and Barbara Windsor challenging the News team with Richard Baker, Angela Rippon and Peter Woods. 1978, his last film for the cinema outside of the Carry On series, in the comedy burlesque version of the classic detective story *The Hound of the Baskervilles* as Sir Henry Baskerville with Peter Cook and Dudley Moore as Sherlock Holmes and Dr Watson.

KENNETH WILLIAMS
(The Undertaker)

Kenneth started in the Theatre as an amateur actor with the Tavistock Repertory Company and was called up in 1944 at the age of 18. After release from the Army in 1948 he joined the Newquay Rep Theatre, which he interspersed with frequent excursions into radio and TV. During the following years he played at a number of theatres throughout the country and performed in many radio plays, in 1952 he played the Angel in *The Wonderful Visit* by H. G. Wells on TV. After playing Slightly in *Peter Pan* in 1952 he went to the Old Vic Theatre, London in the Birmingham Rep Company's production of *Henry VI*. He then played the Dauphin in *Saint Joan* at the Arts Theatre and the St Martin's Theatre, from there he went on to play several parts in Orson Welles' production of *Moby Dick* at the Duke of York's theatre. He appeared as Montgomery in Sandy Wilson's *The Buccaneer* at the Apollo, Maxime in *Hotel Paradiso* at the Winter Garden and Kite in *The Wit To Woo* at the Arts. He was in *Share My Lettuce* and, in 1958 he opened in one of the most exciting productions of *Cinderella* at the Coliseum when he played Portia. Other popular revues followed—*Pieces Of Eight* and *One Over The Eight*. His other West End plays have included the double bill *The Private Ear* and *The Public Eye*, *Gentle Jack*, and he starred in the original production of *Loot* by Joe Orton. Later he was in *Captain Brassbound's Conversion* and *My Fat Friend*. In his film career he played Jack in Peter Brook's production of *The Beggars Opera* followed by Jack Wishart in *The Seekers*. He is well known for his many appearances in the *Carry On...* series of films. His numerous television appearances include *Hancock's Half Hour* (also on radio), and the plays *Catch As Catch Can*, *Misalliance* as well as 52 episodes of *International Cabaret* and *The Kenneth Williams Show*. He is also a frequent story-teller on *Jackanory*. He is a great favourite from such radio series as *Beyond Our Ken*, *Round The Horne*, *The Secret Life Of Kenneth Williams*, *The Betty Witherspoon Show*, *More Secret Life*, *Just A Minute*, *Kenneth Williams Playhouse*, *Oh! Get On With It*, etc., etc.

FORTUNE THEATRE

THE UNDERTAKING

5 December 1979, with June Whitfield and Kenneth Connor at a BBC Radio Christmas Party. On the small screen as a panelist in *Give Us a Clue*, *Star Turn Challenge* and *The Steve Jones Game Show*. October 1979 and Kenneth's last play on the stage in Trevor Baxter's *The Undertaking* as the Undertaker.

84

Autumn 1979, with Lorraine Chase and Miriam Karlin in *The Undertaking*. 1974, recording *A Book at Bedtime: Nightmare Abbey* for the BBC, which was broadcast in 1979.

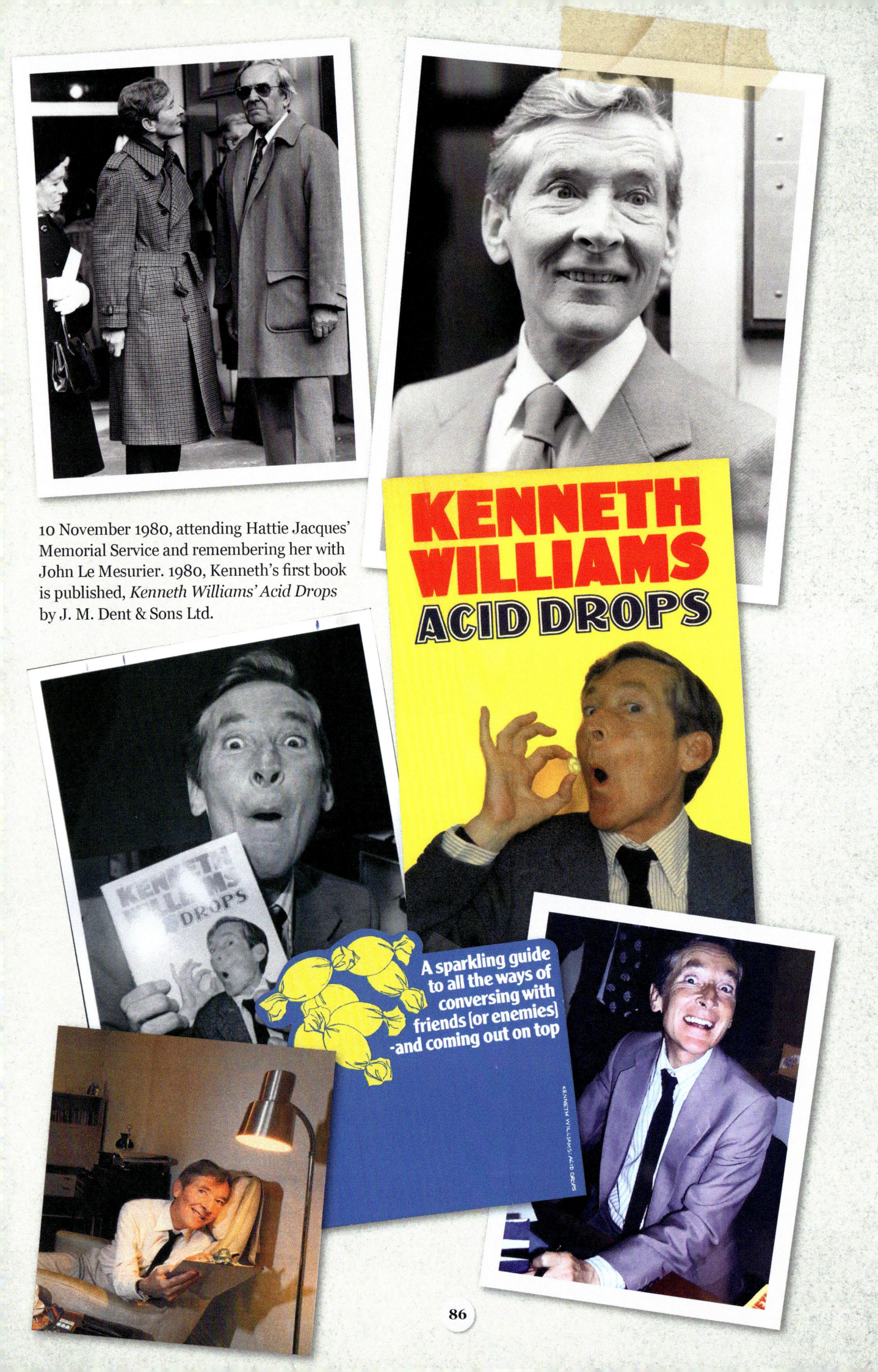

10 November 1980, attending Hattie Jacques' Memorial Service and remembering her with John Le Mesurier. 1980, Kenneth's first book is published, *Kenneth Williams' Acid Drops* by J. M. Dent & Sons Ltd.

KENNETH WILLIAMS ACID DROPS

A sparkling guide to all the ways of conversing with friends (or enemies) –and coming out on top

THE WHIZZKIDS

It looks as if Kenneth here has been trying to count to a billion — that's a million million which looks like this: 1,000,000,000,000! Counting at your fastest you could only get up to about two hundred in one minute and so, at this rate (assuming you could keep it up and go without food, drink, sleep, school and television) it would take you at least 9,512 years before you reached a billion!

1980, *Whizzkids Guide*, a series which was a lighthearted guide for children on how to cope with school life, with Kenneth playing a school kid throughout. 28 February 1982, *Sunday Best*, a religious magazine programme with Kenneth contributing to the lighthearted side and pictured with Peter Sarstedt.

5.35 New series
Willo the Wisp
The Bridegroom
With the voices of
KENNETH WILLIAMS
Written and directed by NICK SPARGO

5.40 Evening News
with Richard Baker
Weatherman

6.0 Regional news magazines and Nationwide

14 September 1981, the debut of *Willo the Wisp*, the animated series based around characters living in Doyley Woods for which Kenneth did all the voices. There was Willo, the narrator; Mavis Cruet, the fairy; Arthur, the caterpillar; Evil Edna, the witch; Carwash, a cat; The Moog, a dog; Twit, a bird and the Beast, a former prince. The creator, writer, director and producer Nicholas Spargo is pictured working on the series.

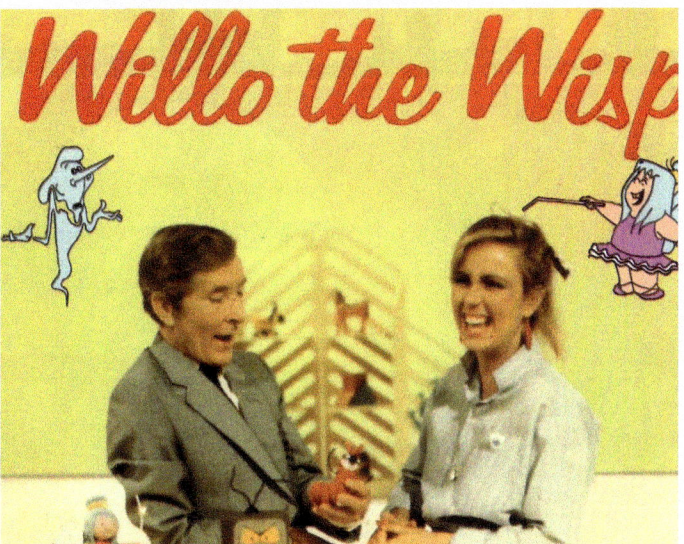

28 October 1982, *Blue Peter*, Kenneth appeared on the children's television programme in conversation with Sarah Greene, who had made characters from *Willo the Wisp* which were featured in that year's *Blue Peter Annual*.

BILL KENWRIGHT & ALAN CLUER present

JOE ORTON'S LOOT

JOAN BLACKHAM · PHILIP MARTIN BROWN
RORY EDWARDS · JOHN MALCOLM
NEIL McCARTHY

DESIGNED BY SAUL RADOMSKY · LIGHTING BY DICK JOHNSON

DIRECTED BY
KENNETH WILLIAMS

A Lyric Studio Theatre, Hammersmith, production

Arts Theatre
Great Newport St. London WC2   01-836 3334

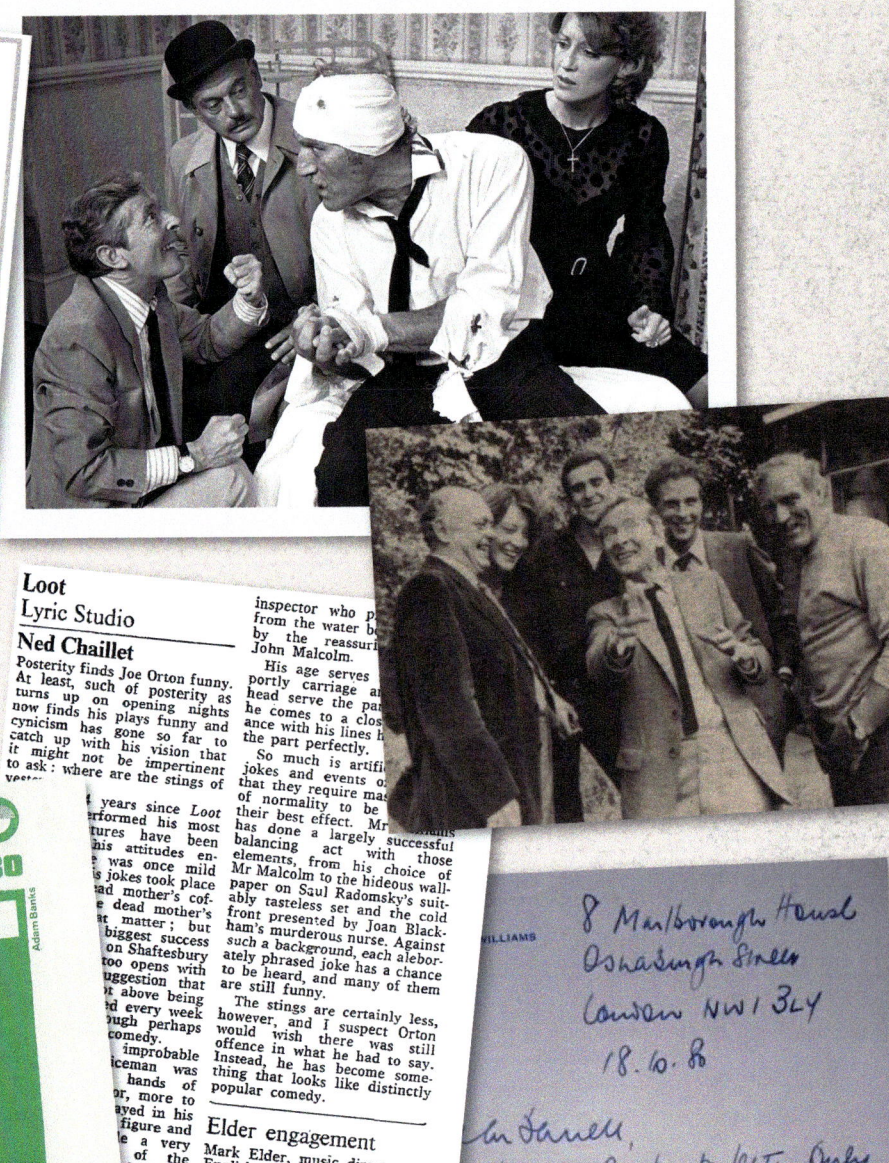

LYRIC STUDIO
11 SEPTEMBER – 4 OCTOBER 1980

LOOT

JOE ORTON

Director KENNETH WILLIAMS · Designer SAUL RADOMSKY · Lighting DICK JOHNSON
JOAN BLACKHAM · RORY EDWARDS · JOHN MALCOLM · NEIL McCARTHY · PHILIP MARTIN BROWN

BOX OFFICE AND INFORMATION: 01 741 2311

Loot
Lyric Studio
Ned Chaillet

Posterity finds Joe Orton funny. At least, such of posterity as turns up on opening nights now finds his plays funny and cynicism has gone so far to catch up with his vision that it might not be impertinent to ask: where are the stings of yesteryear?

[...] years since *Loot* [...] performed his most [...] tures have been [...] his attitudes en- [...] was once mild [...] jokes took place [...] dead mother's c- [...] dead mother's [...] t matter; but [...] biggest success [...] on Shaftesbury [...] too opens with [...] uggestion that [...] above being [...] every week [...] ugh perhaps [...] comedy.

[...] improbable [...] ceman was [...] hands of [...] r, more to [...] ayed in his [...] figure and [...] e a very [...] of the [...] Williams [...] ting the [...] tic sense [...] nbalance [...] police

inspector who p[...] from the water b[...] by the reassuri[...] John Malcolm.

His age serves [...] portly carriage a[...] head serve the pa[...] he comes to a clo[...] ance with his lines h[...] the part perfectly.

So much is artifi[...] jokes and events o[...] that they require mas[...] of normality to be [...] their best effect. Mr [...] has done a largely successful balancing act with those elements, from his choice of paper on Saul Radomsky's suitably tasteless set and the cold front presented by Joan Blackham's murderous nurse. Against such a background, each elaborately phrased joke has a chance to be heard, and many of them are still funny.

The stings are certainly less, however, and I suspect Orton would wish there was still offence in what he had to say. Instead, he has become something that looks like distinctly popular comedy.

Elder engagement

Mark Elder, music director of English National Opera, has been engaged to conduct a new production of *Die Meistersinger* at next year's Bayreuth Festival. Graham Clark sings David.

---

8 Marlborough House
Osnaburgh Street
London NW1 3LY
18.10.80

[handwritten letter]

Autumn 1980, Kenneth's directorial debut for Joe Orton's *Loot* at the Lyric Studio and Arts Theatre and his last stage performance when he went on for one night as Truscott. 5 July 1981, leading the *Jackanory* team on *Star Turn Challenge* with June Whitfield and Peter Jones.

He doesn't own a telly, has never been in love, won't stay with friends and doesn't like people using his loo. He won't accept an MBE, smokes like a chimney and thinks marriage is unnatural. Today as Kenneth Williams, Britain's funniest man, signs copies of his new book Back Drops in Maidstone, SUNDAY gets to grips with the man who says he doesn't believe in happiness

CARRY ON KEN!

"I couldn't write some lurid type of book about my sexual conquests because I don't have any. I never felt the urge"

"Orson Welles told me I would never make it, but he does nothing but ads"

2 January 1981, an appearance on *Tomorrow's World*, demonstrating a watch powered by the heat from his wrist; later, Kenneth has an endoscope down his gullet and stomach at the dinner party focused around dieting and weight problems.

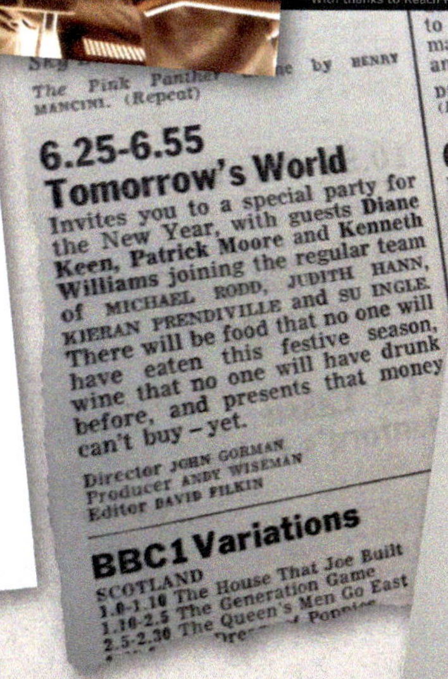

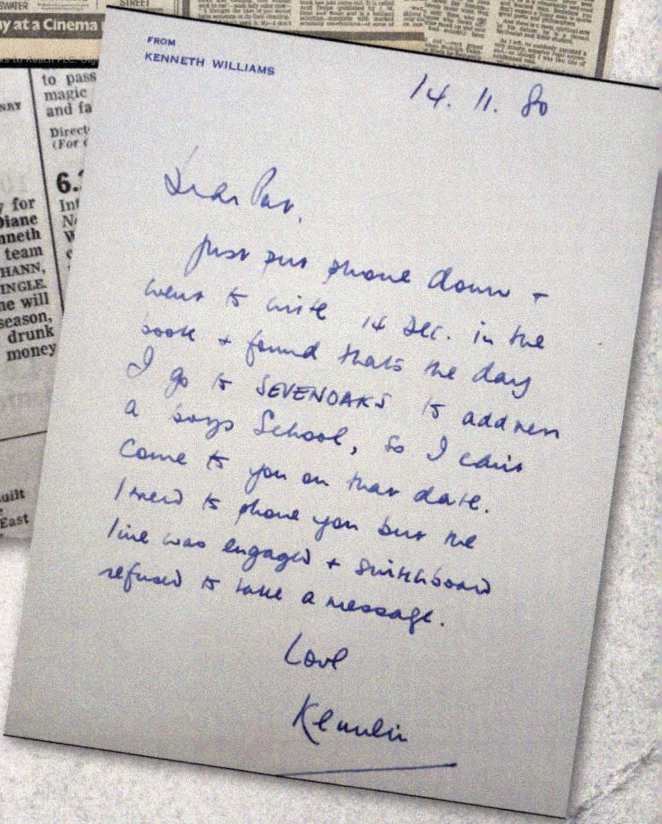

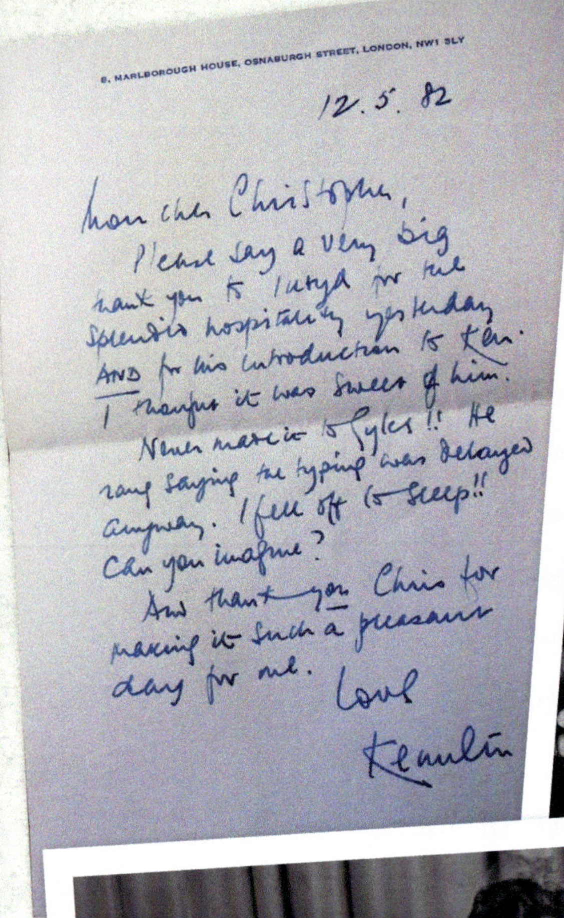

8, MARLBOROUGH HOUSE, OSNABURGH STREET, LONDON, NW1 3LY

12.5.82

Mon cher Christopher,

Please say a very big thank you to Ingrid for the splendid hospitality yesterday AND for his introduction to Ken. I thought it was sweet of him.

Never mind re Tyler!! He rang saying the typing was delayed anyway. I fell off to sleep!! Can you imagine?

And thank you Chris for making it such a pleasant day for me.

Love
Kenneth

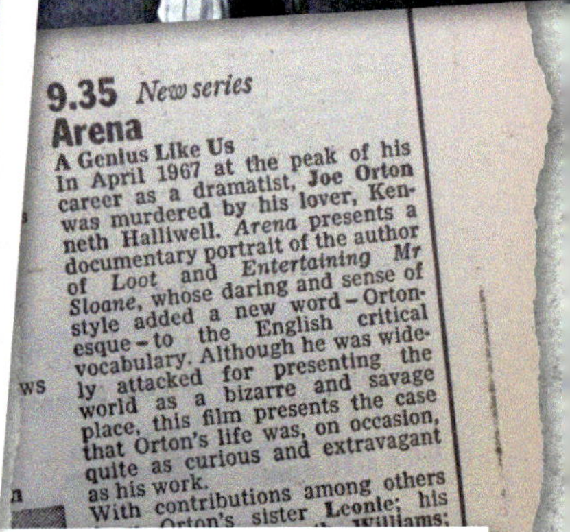

9.35 New series
Arena
A Genius Like Us
In April 1967 at the peak of his career as a dramatist, Joe Orton was murdered by his lover, Kenneth Halliwell. Arena presents a documentary portrait of the author of *Loot* and *Entertaining Mr Sloane*, whose daring and sense of style added a new word — Ortonesque — to the English critical vocabulary. Although he was widely attacked for presenting the world as a bizarre and savage place, this film presents the case that Orton's life was, on occasion, quite as curious and extravagant as his work.
With contributions among others of Orton's sister Leonie; his

1983, *Kenneth Williams' Cabaret*, fun, frippery and frolic furnished by Kenneth and his special guests in this BBC Radio 2 series featuring Pat Coombs, Julie Covington, Peter Hudson and Barbara Jay. 1981, a postcard from Australia where Kenneth travelled to publicise *Acid Drops*.

Kenneth Williams' Cabaret

fun, frippery and frolic furnished by

KENNETH WILLIAMS

and his special guests:

JONATHAN ADAMS	BARBARA JAY
JULIE COVINGTON	PAT COOMBS
LOIS LANE	PETER GOODRIGHT
PETER HUDSON	ISLA ST CLAIR

with

CANTABILE

and

THE BURT RHODES ORCHESTRA

Four half hours of radio cabaret, presented by Kenneth Williams who entertains in his own inimitable style

17.6.81

Arrived 6oc this morning via Singapore & Brunei. City is sparkling in the sunshine. Here to publicise the book etc. Back in July. Hope you aren't moved out yet.

Love
Kenneth

Sydney's unique Opera House at Bennelong Point.

MR & MRS B DOBSON
44 JEYMER DRIVE
GREENFORD
MIDDLESEX
GREAT BRITAIN

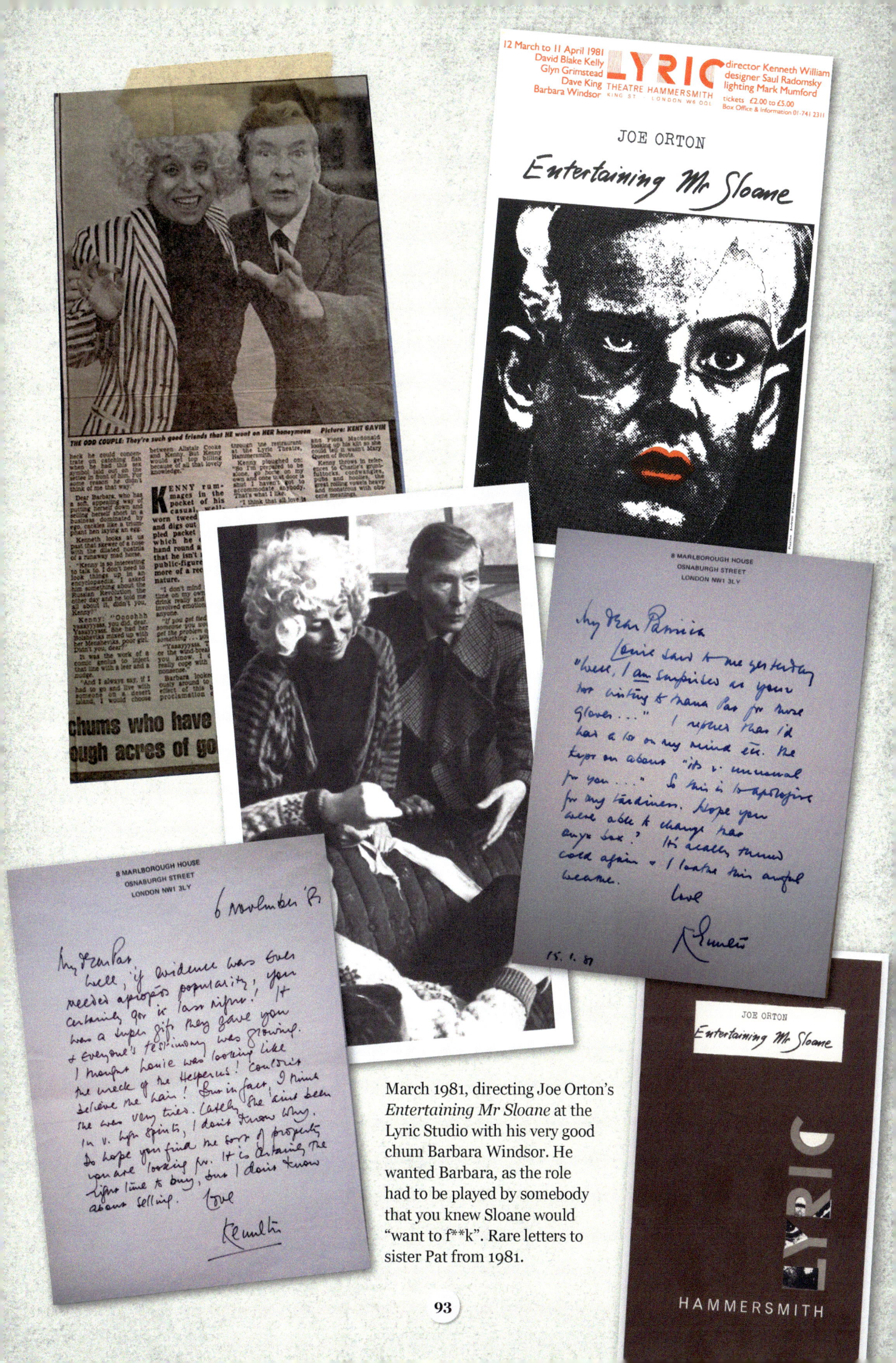

March 1981, directing Joe Orton's *Entertaining Mr Sloane* at the Lyric Studio with his very good chum Barbara Windsor. He wanted Barbara, as the role had to be played by somebody that you knew Sloane would "want to f**k". Rare letters to sister Pat from 1981.

93

1982-83, Kenneth in Dictionary Corner for the Channel 4 game show, *Countdown*, involving word and number puzzles. Hosted by Richard Whiteley. Ted Moult alternated alternated with Kenneth to appear in the Corner.

94

KENNETH WILLIAMS

I.C.M.
388/396 Oxford Street
London W1N 9HE

24. 10. 83

Dear Gail
Yes, the BBC do put out repeats of HANCOCK and ROUND THE HORNE every so often, and BBC Enterprises, London W1A 1AA have a list of programmes which are on disc and cassettes. I've just done AN AUDIENCE WITH KENNETH WILLIAMS which Channel 4 are transmitting in December.

Yours
Kenneth Williams

TELEVISION TODAY

Kenneth Williams, left, being filmed for a new series of the BBC's Comic Roots, in which comedians go back to the scenes of their youth and trace the development of their humour. Here, filming near St Pancras in London, near where Kenneth Williams grew up, are, from the left after Kenneth Williams, producer/director Peter Lee-Wright; second assistant cameraman Jeremy Read; Howard Westwood, first assistant cameraman; lighting cameraman Fred Hamilton, and grips Ian Buckley. Transmission of this programme will be on BBC-1, on September 2.

KENNETH WILLIAMS

His new book, BACK DROPS, pages from a private diary, is published by Dent in early 1983

2 September 1983, the debut of *Comic Roots* on BBC One as Kenneth presents and narrates his early life in and around London. 1983, the publication of Kenneth's second book, *Back Drops: Pages from a Private Diary*, which gave an early insight into the page's of Kenneth's diaries.

95

23 December 1983, *An Audience with Kenneth Williams* (recorded a year previously on 1 December 1982), one of the crowning glories of Kenneth's career bringing together his favourite stories, anecdotes and sketches.

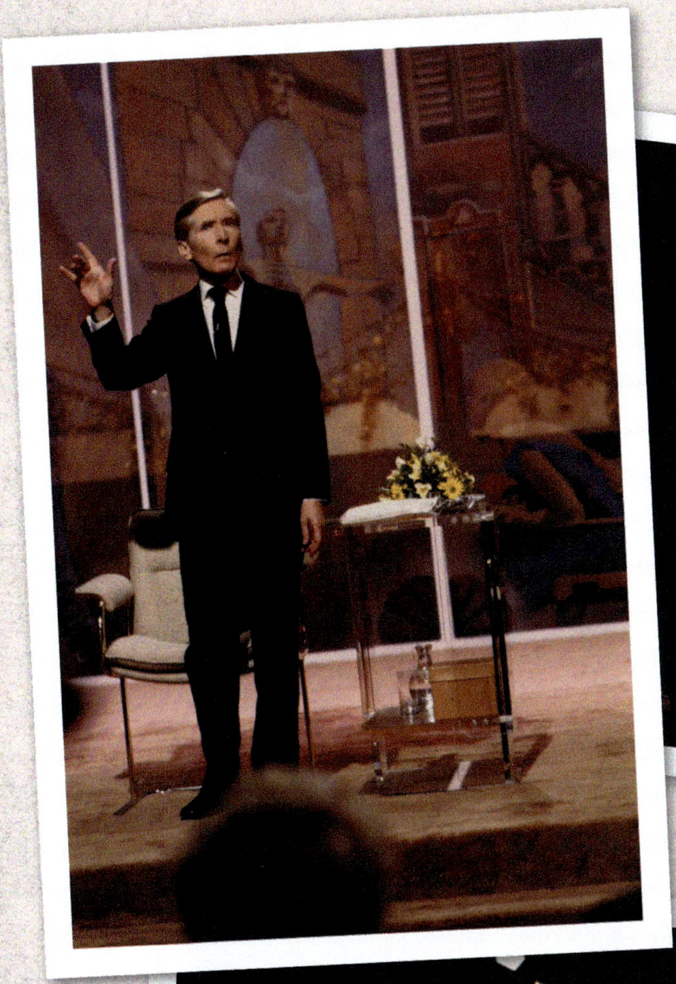

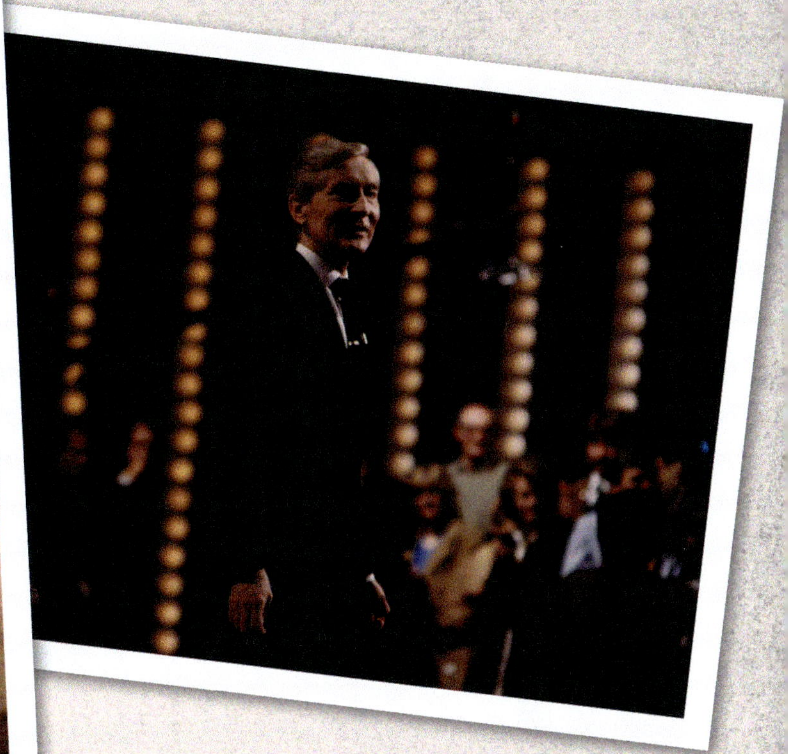

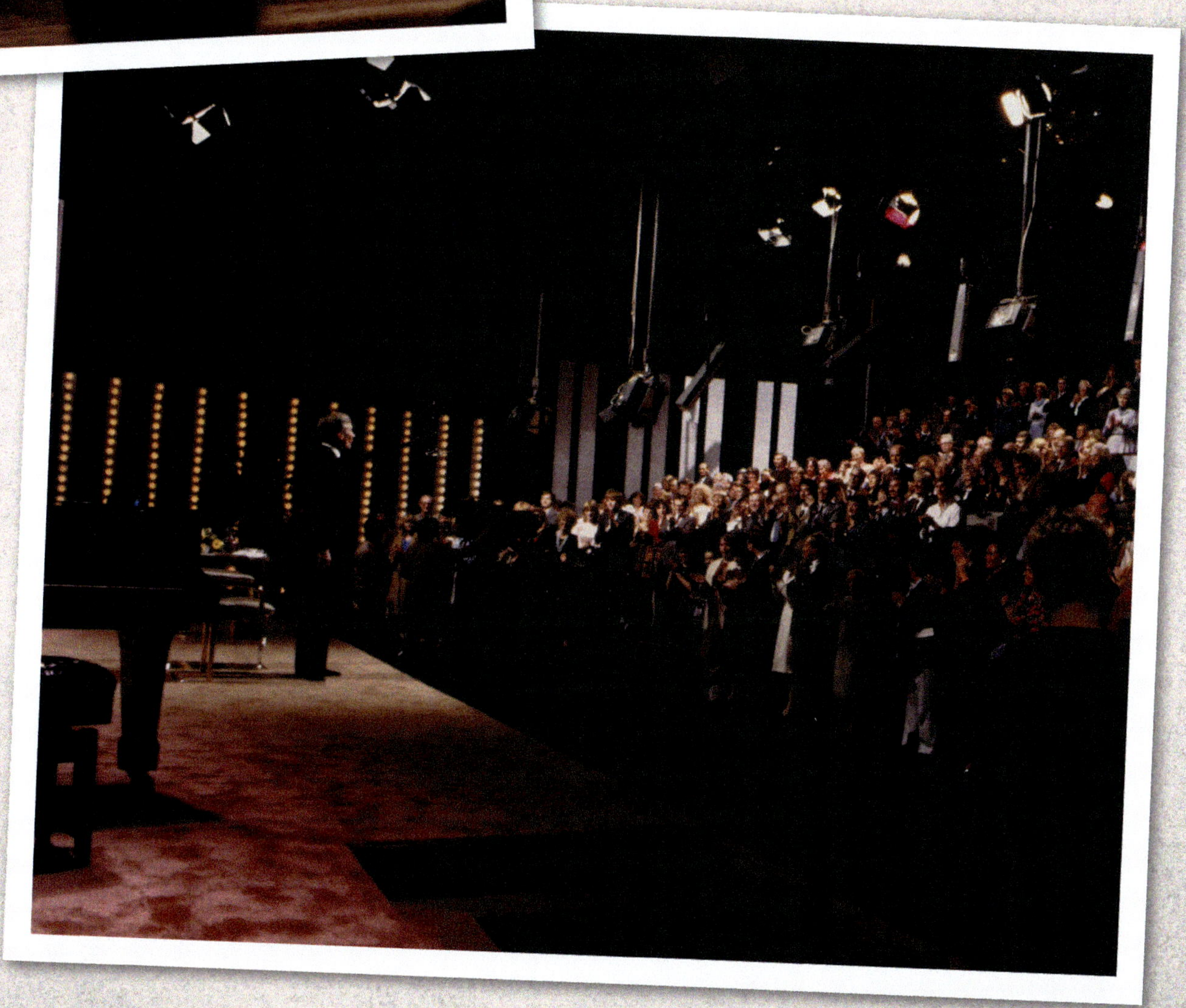

1 December 1982, the after party for the recording of *An Audience with*. From left; with Lorraine Chase; Rona Anderson, Gordon Jackson and Lou; with Nanette Newman; meeting Jean Alexander as Geoffrey Hughes looks on; the Williams family with Lou and Pat; with two dear chums Gordon Jackson and Michael Whittaker; amusing Mary Whitehouse and William Roache and finally in conversation with Dora Bryan.

99

8, MARLBOROUGH HOUSE, OSNABURGH STR...

8 April '83

My dear Patrick

Sweet of you to write so engagingly about the book. I've been going all over the place doing literary dinners and signing sessions. At Birmingham I spoke before Harry Secombe who said of himself (before dieting) "I had more chins than the Hongkong Telephone Directory" which made me laugh. I go to Australia on Wednesday. A week in Sydney on the 'Mike Walsh Show' + then to Melbourne for more book appearances. The Johnson story ("Well Sir, I would give what I have") is in the other book (ACID DROPS). Did you know of COWARD saying to an actor who was mincing on to the stage instead of being properly military "A little more MARTIAL ..... and less SNELGROVE!" I hadn't heard it before! The manager in Harrods (Book dept) told me! Love Kenneth

21 April 1983, with Brian Bury performing *Not An Asp* on *The Mike Walsh Show* – the only existing footage of Kenneth performing a full revue sketch on television. 1983, with Barney Bowe during the filming of the commercial, *Dylon: Making Britain Brighter* and back to *Blue Peter* with Janet Ellis on 10 November 1983.

22 December 1983, *Carry On Laughing's Christmas Classics*, a Christmas special for the *Carry On Laughing* compilation series. Kenneth and Barbara Windsor link choice clips from Carry On days past, while sitting round a Christmas tree – on which Kenneth becomes the fairy on top at the end of the programme.

Summer 1984, *Some You Win*, the entertainment series which took a lighthearted look at life's winners and losers. Kenneth was a guest host with Lulu and Ted Robbins.

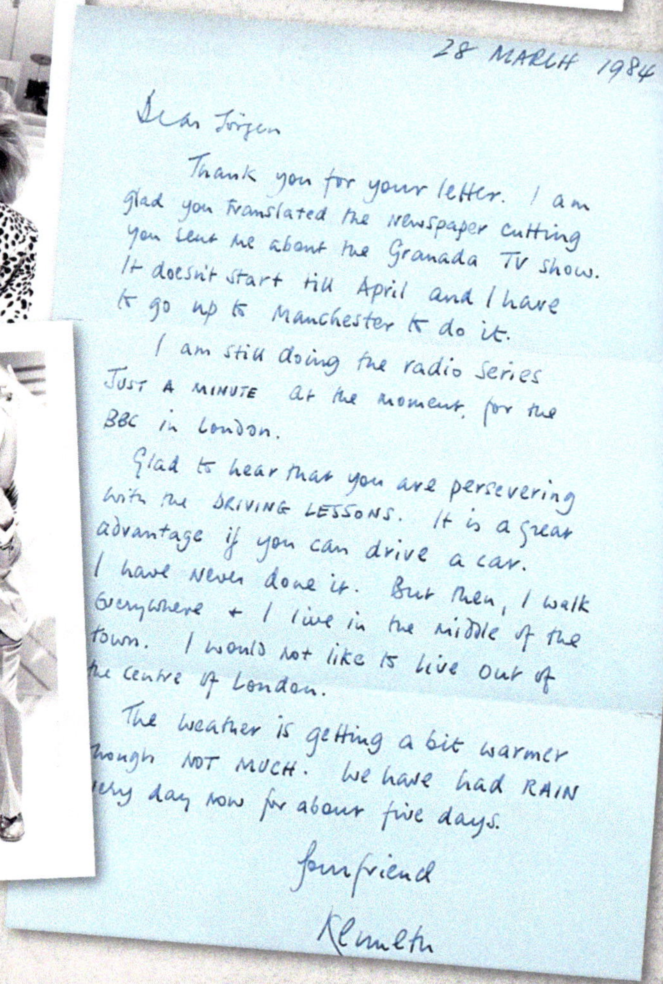

28 MARCH 1984

Dear Jörgen

Thank you for your letter. I am glad you translated the newspaper cutting you sent me about the Granada TV show. It doesn't start till April and I have to go up to Manchester to do it.

I am still doing the radio series JUST A MINUTE at the moment, for the BBC in London.

Glad to hear that you are persevering with the DRIVING LESSONS. It is a great advantage if you can drive a car. I have NEVER done it. But then, I walk everywhere + I live in the middle of the town. I would not like to live out of the centre of London.

The weather is getting a bit warmer though NOT MUCH. We have had RAIN every day now for about five days.

your friend
Kenneth

10.30 Private Lives
Introduced and devised by
Maria Aitken
The last in a series of late-evening conversations in which **Maria Aitken** invites her guests to reminisce and reveal the private memories behind the public face.
Tonight **Kenneth Williams** and **Germaine Greer** compare their personal pleasures and treasures.
Music by PETER SKELLERN with ROBERT WHITE (tenor) and MARIUS MAY (cello)
Assistant producer PETER ESTALL
Director PHILIP CHILVERS
Producer FRANCES WHITAKER

12 June 1984, with host Maria Aitken and fellow guest Germaine Greer on *Private Lives*. 2 August 1984, *Looks Familiar* the nostalgia-based panel chat show with Ernie Wise, Denis Norden and Michael Parkinson. November 1983, release of a new single, *Down in the Woods/Edna's Song* for BBC Records.

8.30
Looks Familiar
DENIS NORDEN
JOHN McCALLUM
KENNETH WILLIAMS
GOOGIE WITHERS
Compiler is Denis Gifford.
FILM RESEARCH CY YOUNG
ASSOCIATE PRODUCER
COLIN WILLIAMS
DIRECTOR/PRODUCER
DAVID CLARK
Thames Television Production

WILLO THE WISP
DOWN IN THE WOODS
Theme from Willo The Wisp
Sung by KENNETH WILLIAMS

KENNETH WILLIAMS

I.C.M.
388/396 Oxford Street
London W1N 9HE

24 October '85

Dear Russ Harraday

JUST WILLIAMS is an autobiography. Quite understand your reservations about the price! It will appear in paperback (FONTANA) in fifteen months time. I thought the hardback price was a bit steep but the publishers have ordered a 3rd reprint so it's doing well.

Yours
Kenneth W.

Carry on Kenneth Williams and Liz Frazer, 'Cross Wits' addicts will be watching your every move at 3.00.

Dr Cullen — Sebastian Breaks
Nicola Freeman — Gabrielle Drake
Barry Hart — Harry Nurmi
Daniel Freeman — Philip Goodhew
Joanna Freeman — Mary Lincoln
Lorraine Baker — Dorothy Brown
Jill Chance — Jane Rossington
WRITER TERRY BARBOUR
STORIES PETER LING
SCRIPT EDITOR KATE HENDERSON
DESIGNER MARTIN DAVEY
DIRECTOR ALISTER HALLUM

7.30 Name That Tune
LIONEL BLAIR
MAGGIE MOONE
Alan Braden and his Orchestra
Music quiz in which a contestant could win £1250, a special prize and a new car. Lionel Blair is host and singer Maggie Moone entertains.

Spring 1985, television shows included *All Star Secrets*, the show in which the stars revealed some of their daft and inconsequential secrets with the help of each other and the studio audience. Kenneth appeared three times. 1985, Kenneth provided a foreword for *Faith Fire and Fun: A Book of Poems* by Bishop Cyril Bulley.

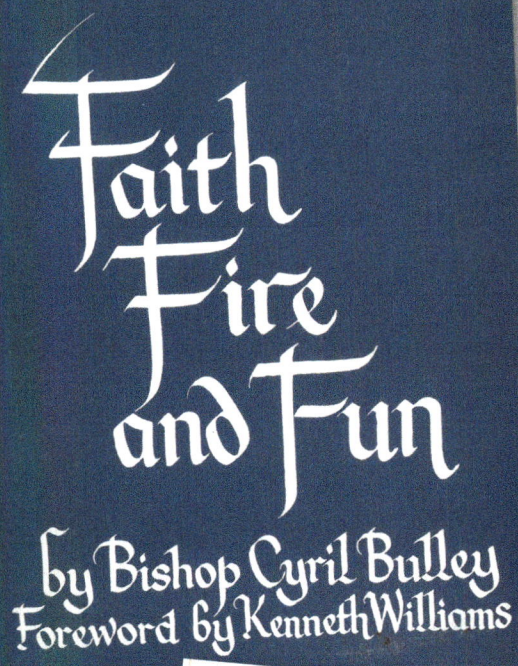

Faith Fire and Fun
by Bishop Cyril Bulley
Foreword by Kenneth Williams

FOREWORD

When Mrs. Runcie visited a children's exhibition of scenes from the nativity recently, she talked to one small boy about his model of the manger in the Bethlehem stable and asked him what he thought about there being no room at the inn for Mary. 'I blame Joseph', he said, 'he should have booked'. The story, which has its adult parallels, illustrates the reaction of modern man to ancient truths.

Every now and again we need reminding that the old is the new, like the masks of comedy and tragedy being the two sides of the same coin. We must remember Eliot's warning: 'We have learned many words but lost THE WORD', and his exhortation: 'We must for ever be rebuilding the temple'. Poets have been endlessly concerned with preserving values, and Chaucer's complaint –

'Man hath made a permutation from right to wrong,
And all is lost through lack of steadfastness . . .'

is another warning for us to go back and look again at what Faith has taught us. Something may look like a battered old coal scuttle but hard work and elbow grease can reveal burnished copper and a valuable antique. Enlightenment can come gravely costumed or in cap and bells and an open mind welcomes both as easily as children entertain a new and lively idea. Cyril Bulley has captured the two facets in this collection of poems. He is a man who has rung bells many times in his life calling us to prayer, and here he has gathered his carillons to remind us that they can call seriously and they can call merrily. Of one of his books Montaigne wrote: 'I have gathered a posy of other men's flowers and only the thread that binds them is my own', but I fancy Dr. Bulley would echo George Herbert's lines:

'I got me flowers to strew Thy way,
I got me boughs off many a tree,
But Thou wast up by break of day,
And brought Thy sweets along with Thee'.

KENNETH WILLIAMS

Autumn 1985, as the voice of the computer SID in *Galloping Galaxies*, a comedy series set in the 25th Century. 1985, as the Genie of the Peas in the four film series *So You Want Your Shop to Be a Success?* and in a voice over session with Simon Pounds.

TAKE 3

That two-faced Kenneth Williams is always telling tall stories. But you can believe every word when he owns up to some 'All Star Secrets' at 7.15

Solitary Confinement

28 September 1981, Kenneth and mother Lou with her WRVS medal, photographed by Terence Donovan and commissioned by Michael Whittaker. 1985, *Just Williams*, Kenneth's autobiography is published with an account of his life up to 1975.

7.2.86

Dear Andrew
I haven't got a television set so I don't know about this puppet who's using my voice, but it sounds so banal I doubt if it's worth worrying about.

Yours
Kenneth

June 1986, the publication of *I Only I Have to Close My Eyes*, a children's book by Kenneth about a small boy who dreams up wonderful worlds in which he plays many roles. Beverlie Manson provided the illustrations and they are seen together here in a book signing, on a Saturday morning, in the window of Liberty.

Best wishes David
Kenneth Williams

4.15 James and the Giant Peach
by ROALD DAHL
Told by Kenneth Williams
for *Jackanory*
Today: James meets the Creatures in the Peach.

107

4.25 Bananaman
Harbour of Lost Ships with the voices of

24 March **MONDAY TV**

side tonight – co-host Peter Cook, Dudley Fox, Kenneth Williams and Phil Collins
0 pm Joan Rivers: Can We Talk?

11.35 Télé-Journal

Letter 1 (handwritten)

KENNETH WILLIAMS
I.C.M.
388/396 Oxford Street
London W1N 9HE

Marlborough House
27. 2. 86

Dear Chris & Lloyd

It's been a HELL of a year so far! I went into Charing X Hosp. for Gastroscopy. They found ULCER & I've been put on pills for 6 weeks before another Gastroscopy. Came out in time to look after Louie, she'd FALLEN in the street. Nursed her for 3 weeks & then she collapsed in the flat + then got her into UCH. So I'm visiting there every day! Trying desperately to see social worker here about getting her into an Old People's Home 'cos I can't cope any more. Sweet of you to send such a lovely Birthday Gift!! I NEEDED a new flannel I can tell you! Came just in time.
Love
Kenneth

April 1986, Kenneth is a guest host for three shows alternating with Sue Lawley for *Wogan*, the talk show hosted by Terry Wogan.

CARRY ON CAMPING

Page 12—New Musical Express 16th August, 1986

Is Kenneth Williams the greatest living Englishman? He's certainly the foremost celibate comedian of our times. JOHN McCREADY meets the comic who prefers poetry to people. Photos: NICK WHITE.

AT 60, Kenneth Williams has decided it's time to stop messing about.

He has, he insists, retired and a canny pension plan ensures that he no longer needs to work.

"I've just turned down an advertisement for Australian champagne for which I would have earned £50,000. The script had me sitting on a beach and kicks sand in my face and I say I'm terribly English too. Frankly, with a glass of XYZ, I should care... Of course it's racist rubbish. It assumes that all Englishmen are wonderfully cultured and all Australians are brainless bruisers. You'll find many more uncultured yobs on the football terraces of England. No, I only do what I want to do."

AT THE offices of his publishers in central London Kenneth Williams toys with a cigarette.

The celibate who has lived alone with his books, the boy whose best friends were "slim volumes of poetry" draws on his fag with the air of a ship-wrecked sailor. "My friends were "slim volumes of poetry", "the imagination was king and artists were heroes" has transcended his humble origins. It's perhaps all he wanted. A host of golden daffodils must have been hard to find just off London's Caledonian Road where he was born.

We talk about his life. In a standard BBC English which he insists was self-taught. "I've had no elocution lessons. But you must remember that I'd never have got into the theatre with my dreadful cockney accent" — he agrees that the biographical pages of Just Williams and Backdrops reveal a talent for writing, straight acting (Williams spent a virtual lifetime in the theatre proper before he was hi-jacked by Round The Horne, Hancock and Carry On) and messing about which has never been handled by wit.

"Yes, of course that's true, but then I've come to regard the riches of this world as total dross. Even in the past I've only worked to get what gets me by."

Those magnificent nostrils dilate. They compete for top billing with small blue eyes on a face which Kenneth's life as a bachelor boy has kept relatively free of wrinkles. Its sight blurs and he looks like an ageing 30 year old in middle management. "I suppose my appearance shows I've lived quite happily without a wife or family."

Each question is answered thoughtfully and intelligently. Today, the public persona "that cunt on the telly", the temporary Wogan host gossiping gaily about this and that — has been given the day off.

The lisp any evidence of the surroundings play their part. He refers to books and authors, quoting freely and loudly and explain. Cobley, Captain Fearless, Judge Burke, Dr Tinkle and The Khasi Of Kalabar are largely out to lunch. Today, Kenneth Williams has decided he will be "himself", the respected thespian, the contemplative elder statesman of business, the Englishman at leisure, parting with his three score years and facing his faith.

Does death worry Kenneth?

"No, not in the least, though I want the Keats thing — 'ceasing upon the midnight with no pain'. Dr Tinkle of the Caledonian Road was stuck up the arse and winding up in some hospital unit fading away like an old fart is frightening, yes."

Mark Antony: "We've just had word from Egypt. Ptolemy's raised an army and is marching on Alexandria"
Caesar: (K.W.) "Oh dear! And what about Cleopatra? Is she mustered?"
Mark: "Well, I have heard one or two stories..."
Excerpt from Carry On Cleo (1964).

LIKE A line full of dirty washing, the Carry Ons must be aired. Kenneth Williams appeared in 24 of them — more than anybody else, including those such as Sid James and Barbara Windsor who are perhaps more closely associated with the genre. The fact that he will be remembered for these rather than his Shavian leads and appearances in razor-edged highbrow smut like Joe Orton's Loot doesn't appear to bother him.

"I don't care what I'm remembered for. Why should anybody remember me? The idea that you should be remembered at all after you've gone is preposterous."

Are you aware of how popular they still are, Kenneth?

"Oh, yes, but these young people will grow out of them. When I say 'legend I never dreamed they'd become cult pieces. I thought they were rather cheap films which would have a vogue. But they weren't a bit wide, which was nice. They had an honest vulgarity.

"But I think they lost their way. The first, Carry On Sergeant, was good, a good story, but with the second, Carry On Nurse, they didn't really bother with the story. They lined up a whole series of gags until the last one, where a man's temperature is taken with a daffodil up his backside. Of course, it got the biggest laugh of the film and from that was it, the stories went out of the window..." Kenneth tells some Carry On stories but I shan't repeat them — I'm sure you'll already have heard them. I know what you're interested in.

Billy (schoolboy): "Didn't you know sir? Girls is different from men!"
Milton (K.W., teacher): "I'm not interested in the girl down your street."
Irene: "Well, you're in the minority. Only last Saturday night..."
Milton: "Be quiet. This has nothing to do with Romeo and Juliet..."
Excerpt from Carry On Teacher (1959).

KENNETH WILLIAMS who, in character of course, was once a weak man (and once a week's enough for any man) says he has never shared his life, his home, his bed or his books with anyone.

"I don't want to share. I don't like the idea of anyone having my books or using my bathroom. I really do not want people in my abode. I don't like it. It's essentially a private place. And the idea of ablutions and whatever is all bound up with that."

Unlike his weak-willed potential spiritual understudy, Steven Morrissey (a purveyor incidentally of what Kenneth Williams refers to as a "formless din"), the comic actor has observed his self-imposed celibate code to the letter. "The more I see of the complicated and sometimes tragic nature of people's liaisons, the more I think, I'm glad I'm out of it." The last six words are immaculately emphasised.

"Oh, undoubtedly, yes. It's been a very smooth life. He's said, 'You're not much cop at living how a man should live — there won't be any issue of the loins. We'd better give you some compensation. We'll make you a performer.' Yes, that's it."

We talk of other performers we both admire, Ted Ray, Frankie Howerd and Les Dawson, performers Kenneth sees on his mum Louisa's telly when he visits (he doesn't own a television set himself). He confesses he knows nothing of the new breed, the Spitting Images and The Young Ones, and this man who inexplicably seems to guard, even hide, a peerless ability to initiate laughter with a simple gesture or a mere modulation of that multi-toned voice tells me: "I'm not really interested in comedy overmuch. I find myself laughing less and less. But then I always was a serious person. I've loved poetry, books and theatre, judging by the sprightly way he paced down Wellbeck Street after our conversation, that day is thankfully a long way off.

'Till then, I doubt that this wonderful Kenneth Williams, as great an Englishman as any of the poets and writers he reveres, can stop himself from messing about.

Letter 2 (handwritten)

KENNETH WILLIAMS
I.C.M.
388/396 Oxford Street
London W1N 9HE

26. 2. 86

Dear Susan
Sorry, don't approve of fan clubs. The answers to all your questions are in the biography JUST WILLIAMS. Hope you're keeping warm in this fearful weather!
Yours
Kenneth

5 November THURSDAY TV

6.00 World Cup Cricket
Second Semi-final from Bombay, India
TONY GUBBA introduces highlights of the second semi-final and the line-up for the final to be played in Calcutta on Sunday.
Commentators in India
TONY LEWIS
RAY ILLINGWORTH
JACK BANNISTER
Television presentation
DDI, India
Producer KEITH MACKENZIE

NEW SERIES
6.50 Cover to Cover
First of 20 programmes
As the bookshops stock up for Christmas the book review programme returns with the pick of the autumn lists.
This week Jill Neville is joined by Victoria Glendinning, Jack Klaff and Kenneth Williams to discuss Oscar Wilde by Richard Ellman, Dan Jacobson's novel Her Story, and Tales of Natural and Unnatural Catastrophes, a new collection of short stories by this week's guest author Patricia Highsmith; plus a look at the year's best science fiction and fantasy novels.

Kenneth Williams on Wilde – nothing to do BBC2, 6.50pm Cover to C

7.20-8.00 Thinking Aloud
'Most literature has been made by the disinherited or the exiled. Both states fix the attention upon experience and thus on the need to redeem it from oblivion, to hold it tight in the dark.'

Friday's programme

12.15pm Desert Island Discs
The castaway this week is **Kenneth Williams**, who, for 40 years, has occupied a unique place on stage, screen and radio. In conversation with **Michael Parkinson**, he recalls his long career which has ranged from working on radio classics like *Hancock's Half Hour* and *Round the Horne* to being a regular member of the cast in the *Carry On* films.
He chooses the eight records he would take to the mythical island.
Programme created by ROY PLOMLEY
Producer RAY ABBOTT. Stereo
(Re-broadcast on Friday at 9.5am)

HEAR THIS!
RADIO HIGHLIGHTS BY DAVID GILLARD

Just Williams

R4 Kenneth Williams believes in the Wordsworthian theory that 'the child is father of the man'. "We don't change that much — there are certain characteristics that stay with us for the rest of our lives,' he says. 'All we do is to acquire certain mechanisms under which they can operate.'
You certainly wouldn't find it too difficult to recognise the young Williams from his school reports. 'Would do even better if he did less talking during classes,' says one from 1931, when he was only 5 — a clear indication of the prowess he was later to display in *Just a Minute*.
This week he looks at those old reports – 'I keep everything. I have an absolute reverence for papers' – for *Could Do Better* (Wednesday 11.02am LW), the first of a new series in which personalities like Janet Street-Porter, Terence Stamp, comedian Stephen Fry and union leader Brenda Dean will recall the so-called 'best days of their lives' with the aid of their teachers' assessments.
Kenneth found his London County Council schooling 'terribly boring. I didn't learn any real wisdom. The old LCC system was good if you were prepared to co-operate; I wasn't. But the masters could be perceptive. One wrote in my report: "Quick to grasp the bones of a subject, slow to develop them." And that's true of me to this day.'
'Everything I've learnt has come through acting – it was the theatre that woke me up,' he says. 'I never sat an examination, never had to prove anything. The old LCC system was good if you were prepared to co-operate; I wasn't. But the masters could be perceptive.'
His reports seem to belie his memory, with high marks for most subjects and 'excellent' written beside many. At his father's insistence that he should 'have a trade' he later went to the LCC School of Photo-Engraving and Lithography and did well in subjects like metal printing and etching. When the school was evacuated to Bicester he spent much of his time on an allotment, 'digging for victory'.
But an early talent for acting was spotted and he appeared in a school production of Thackeray's *The Rose and the Ring* – 'in drag' as Princess Angelica. A theatrical career was to come now. Here he brings together the two great mythical figures of Western literature, the man of intellect and sensual man. It's a marvellous piece of craftsmanship and it punctures both

Kenneth in class: at infants' school (below, third from left, front row); during the war (left)

Hits from misses
R2 Memorable hits from unmemorable flops, or not very successful shows — at least, that's the idea behind Dick Vosburgh's new series

Dance of death
R1 History is made when Radio 1 airs its first play on's *Dancing with*

KENNETH WILLIAMS

I.C.M.
388/396 Oxford Street
London W1N 9HE

27 May '87

Dear Stephen

No I don't know of any Carry On film being made or anything about a Carry On book. The first is doubtless just another rumour + the second probably a load of rubbish. Hope you are keeping well in this election period: the excitement is underwhelming isn't it?

Yours
Kenneth

A selection from Kenneth's later years including a second appearance on *Desert Island Discs* on 26 July 1987, in conversation with Michael Parkinson.

March–April 1988, Kenneth's final radio appearance on *The Spinners and Friends* recorded 7 March. 9 April, his final photo session for a repackaged edition of his book *Acid Drops*.

15 April 1988, Kenneth was found dead in his bed by his mother Lou. The coroner recorded an open verdict.

16 April 1988, news of Kenneth's death, and subsequent funeral on 22 April, made the headlines in the papers along with the outcome of the inquest in June.

Carry On star Ken died from overdose

INQUEST'S OPEN VERDICT AS BARBARA LEAVES IN TEARS SAYING: IT MUST HAVE BEEN AN ACCIDENT

DAILY EXPRESS Friday June 17 1988

By Express Reporter KIM WILLSHER

COMEDY star Kenneth Williams left a mystery yesterday after an inquest heard that he had died from an overdose of sleeping pills.

It was not certain whether the overdose was deliberate or accidental, and an open verdict was recorded.

But after the hearing pathologist Dr Christopher Pease said: "It is possible he could have accidentally overdosed but probably not likely."

St Pancras coroner's court heard Kenneth had been in extreme pain for 18 months because of a stomach ulcer and had been due to have an operation.

He died from an overdose of a barbiturate called sodium amylobarbitone.

The Carry On star's GP Dr Carlos Clarke, told the hearing he prescribed tablets for the ulcer and sleeping pills — but not those from which he had died.

Coroner Dr John Elliott said: "Where Mr Williams would have got these from we won't be able to establish and there is no indication as to why he should have taken this overdose and therefore I record an open verdict."

Later Dr Pease said: "He was in a great deal of pain with his ulcer. It is possible he could have accidently overdosed but probably not likely."

"It's unlikely anyone takes a sizeable amount of tablets accidentally if they are compos mentis. Then again if you are in a large amount of pain you have a different perception of what is right."

Carry On star Barbara Windsor left the inquest in tears. She said: "There is absolutely no question of him doing it deliberately. That is stupid. It was an accident I am 100 per cent sure of it."

She said she saw Kenneth a week before his death and was looking forward to an operation and to having a holiday.

Barbara, who sat through the hearing with the sister, Pat, and Paul Richardson, a close friend of the family, added: "He was just wonderful we loved him so much. I still miss him and I am grieving for him."

Williams: Ulcer
Kenneth, 62, was found dead

Carry on Kenneth dies after op scare

Saturday, April 16, 1988 20p

Kenneth ... he needed surgery to cure an ulcer

By SHAN LANCASTER

CARRY ON star Kenneth Williams—found dead in his bed yesterday—spent his last days in fear of a stomach operation.

Doctors told Kenneth, a heavy smoker, he needed surgery to cure a stomach ulcer.

Yesterday his agent Michael Anderson, an old friend, said he knew 62-year-old Kenneth on Thursday. Ray Cooney booked him to play opposite Ian McKellen in Loot, which opens in April.

He said: "Kenneth was not himself at all."

He said he had been told he needed an operation for his ulcer and he didn't fancy it.

"Although he looked rough, he didn't give the impression he was ill."

Kenneth had always said he didn't want to "hang about" past the age of 65.

He was King of Carry On
Pages 4 and 5

But fellow Carry On actor Charles Hawtrey said: "I am most surprised." He added: "I don't know. Kenneth's was just humour."

Continued on Page Four

Kenneth the comic genius is dead at 62

By STEVE ABSALOM and PAUL CHARMAN

CARRY ON star Kenneth Williams, one of Britain's best-loved comics, died at his home yesterday of a suspected heart attack.

Williams, 62, was found dead in bed at his flat in London's Regent's Park by his 87-year-old mother Louise.

A spokesman for the star's agent, Michael Anderson, said that Williams's death came "as a complete shock to everyone who knew him."

He added: "We were only talking to him yesterday and he seemed fine. The only illness we know of was in March last year when he went into hospital for something minor.

"We believe he died of a heart attack. His mother, to whom he was devoted, is terribly upset."

The spokesman said the comic had not been overworking. He was doing radio work like always. Kenneth always took things fairly easy. There were no signs of heart trouble in the past.

"It is a terrible loss. He was so well loved by showbusiness people and by the public. He was always proud of the fact that the public loved him so much."

Williams made his name in radio, with shows such as Round The Horn with Kenneth Horne.

But it was the Carry On

Jack Tinker — Page 17

Turn to Page 2, Col. 1

Kenneth Williams is found dead

By Jane Thynne, Media Correspondent

KENNETH WILLIAMS, star of the Carry On films and Round The Horne and a superlative performer on BBC's Just a Minute, died yesterday in his sleep. He was 62.

He was found in his central London flat, where he lived alone, by his 87-year-old mother, Mrs Louisa Williams, who lives with his sister in the same block.

He had been undergoing treatment for stomach ulcers. According to friends, Williams, who had often said that he did not want to live beyond 65, had recently lost weight.

Kenneth Williams had made 22 Carry On films and had been due to start shooting the next film in the series later this year. More recently he had hosted the Terry Wogan Show and in 1980 directed Loot by his friend Joe Orton.

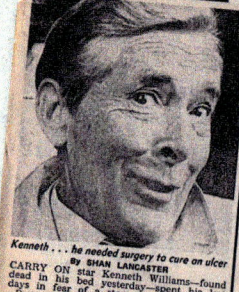

He had also written an autobiography, Acid Drops, in which he said his nasal camp and his motto "Stop messing about" would never go out of fashion.

Frank[...] the [...] day that [...] wanted [...]

Gordon [...] said Wil[...] a more [...] acter. [...] and [...]

Obituary: Kenneth Williams

A rich and lonely voice

Kenneth Williams ... variations on a single comic theme

KENNETH Williams has died at the age of 62. With his nasal, quickfire patter, a voice which swooped in overarticulated emphases upon key words, those flared nostrils and eyebrows rising and falling to mark another of his gleeful double entendres, he became one of the most distinguished post-war British comedians. Although he graduated from army revues with the likes of Stanley Baxter to a career as a star of 22 Carry On Films, the West End stage and television, Williams essentially presented a series of elegant variations upon a single comic theme.

He was always the personification of a form of homosexual camp. He specialised in suave innuendo, in the verbal leer and what would now be termed gay banter.

Williams was born into the working classes but never, he would later say, felt himself less than several cuts above this station. He made his London debut as Slightly in Peter Pan. Early on Kenneth Tynan called him "a blond young prig".

But Williams was to advance beyond that status as an early feed to Tony Hancock and in the most homophobic of times he became a national radio celebrity as one of the two gay chatterers, Julian and Sandy, in Round The Horne. Williams evidently revelled in the opportunities to flaunt that rich voice. And he did so further and more sharply in two famous radio and stage revues, Share My Lettuce and Pieces Of Eight, in the late Fifties, when this form of entertainment was reaching its last phase of popularity. Although he acted notably in straight roles — as the Dauphin in Shaw's St Joan and Julian in Peter Shaffer's The Private Ear And The Public Eye — Williams was too vivid a character and too comical to be so confined. In Just A Minute, on radio, and Introducing Cabaret, on TV, he could play himself to the high manner born.

In private life he seems to have conformed to cliché and been a melancholic comedian who regretted his sexual orientation and whose considerable intelligence was vitiated by clinging neuroses. He lived alone, close to his mother, in a London flat, read widely, was fearful of going abroad and of inviting friends home for fear that they would have need to put their bottoms upon his lavatory seats. Sexual contact was, he believed, the sure route to germs and disease.

Joe Orton, the playwright, a close friend of Williams, observed his loneliness and commented in his diaries: "His only outlet is exhibiting his extremely funny personality in front of an audience and when he isn't doing this he's a very sad man indeed."

Nicholas de Jongh

Kenneth Williams, born February 22 1926. Died April 15

SECRET FUNERAL CARRY ON KEN

Handful of mourners and no flowers

By ROB SKELLON

THE funeral of Carry On star Kenneth Williams has been held in secret, it was revealed yesterday.

Only his treasured mother Louisa, 87, and a handful of close friends and relatives attended the cremation service. There were no flowers and not even a memorial plaque for the 62-year-old comic.

And the 30-minute service, held on Thursday, was so hush-hush that many of the staff at London's St Marylebone Crematorium did not know it was taking place.

Professionals star Gordon Jackson, one of those present, said yesterday: "It was the way Kenneth wanted it — simple and intensely private.

"He was obsessed with personal privacy."

The mourners included Carry On co-star Barbara Windsor, Baker, actress Maggie Smith, and Kenneth's sister Pat.

Barbara said: "It was a beautiful service."

Kenneth was found dead by his mother a week ago at his Marylebone flat, which adjoins hers.

Tests to reveal the cause of his death are still not complete.

Punks tamed by Maggie

A BOSS ordered two girl workers to change their punk hairstyles — because Maggie Thatcher was visiting their factory.

Becky Bell, 22, and Chris Cumberland, 20, had to comb out their spiky locks just hours before the Prime Minister opened the £3 million extension at Bil borough, Nottingham.

29 September 1988, Kenneth's Memorial Service was held at St Paul's (The Actors' Church) in Covent Garden to celebrate his life.

In laughing memory of Ken Williams...

By RICHARD WALLACE

WITH a string of risque jokes, poems and songs, the world of showbusiness yesterday said farewell to Kenneth Williams.

There was no solemnity at the memorial service to the 62-year-old Carry On star, who died earlier this year.

Instead there was laughter and applause as such celebrities as Stanley Baxter, Gordon Jackson, Derek Nimmo and Barbara Windsor celebrated his career.

They were among 200 people at St Paul's, the actors' church, in Covent Garden.

Many wept tears of laughter as Lance Percival mimicked some of Williams's catchphrases. He said later: "Kenneth has stopped 'messin' about" but his characters will linger with us for years.'

Ned Sherrin told the congregation that Williams was 'one of the most vividly theatrical figures of our time'. And actresses Sheila Hancock and Eileen Atkins read two of the star's favourite poems — Boy Actor by Noel Coward and T.S. Eliot's The Waste Land.

Life-long friend and fellow Carry-On star Barbara Windsor sang the music-hall song The Boy I Love Is Up In The Gallery, and Kenneth Connor, who also appeared in many of the classic British film comedies, sang Williams's own version of Auld Lang Syne — in pidgin French.

Miss Windsor said afterwards: 'This was no time to be sad. We wanted to say goodbye to Kenny as he would have wanted.'

Williams's 87-year-old mother, Louisa, who found him dead from an overdose of sleeping pills in April, said of the service: 'It was beautiful. I know he would have loved it.'

Also in church were two beneficiaries of Williams's £540,000 will — his godson, Robert Chiddell, 12, and businessman Michael Whittaker.

Robert said after the service that he had been surprised to be left the money. 'Williams,' he added, 'was a nice man who was good fun and made me laugh.'

Robert Chiddell: 'Kenneth was good fun'
Williams's mother
... and Liz Fraser

Happy farewell to star

CARRY ON LAUGHING

Farewell smiles ... Carry On co-stars Barbara Windsor and Liz Fraser yesterday

Kenneth Williams ... extrovert

'It's what Kenneth would have wanted'

CARRY ON comedy stars paid their final tribute to Kenneth Williams yesterday ... and said it were determined to make it a happy farewell.

Barbara Windsor, who went to St Paul's Church in London's Covent Garden, said: 'Crying is no celebration the said.'

'We will have a nice time thinking about Kenneth and we will have a good job.'

'It's what he would have wanted.'

Memories ... Kenneth's mum Louisa
Robert ... inherited £½ million

THE TIMES FRIDAY SEPTEMBER 30 1988

Stars' laughter celebrates a life

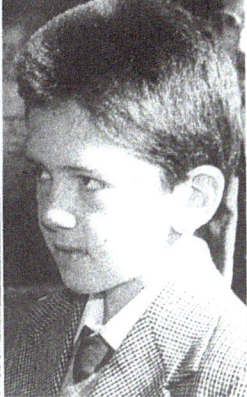

Guests at the memorial service included Robert Chiddell (right) the actor's godson, who was left a substantial amount of money and (clockwise from top left) Gordon Jackson, Barbara Windsor, Stanley Baxter and Kenneth Connor.

St Paul's, Covent Garden, the "actors' church", rang to the laughter and applause yesterday of friends of Kenneth Williams, the comedian.

The star of the Carry On films, famous for his imitations and nasal cackle, was found dead in his flat in April from an overdose of sleeping pills. An open verdict was recorded at his inquest. He was 62.

But there was to be no mourning at his memorial service. Barbara Windsor, the actress, a lifelong friend and Carry On colleague, said: "Today is a celebration day. There will be no tears. We will have a nice time thinking about Kenneth and we will have a big laugh."

Derek Nimmo, so often the foil to Kenneth Williams on the radio panel game Just A Minute, said during the service: "He was deeply shy yet extrovert beyond belief. He was a sensitive scholar and yet a very naughty schoolboy". The 200 guests at the church included Stanley Baxter and Kenneth Connor, the comedian, Sheila Hancock and Eileen Atkins, the actresses, Gordon Jackson, the actor, and Nicholas Parsons, chairman of Just a Minute.

Mr Williams's mother, Louisa, aged 87, arrived on the arm of his sister, Pat. Mr Nimmo said Mrs Williams had sat in the same seat for every performance of Just A Minute for the past 20 years.

Mr Williams first became known for his radio parts in shows such as Beyond Our Ken, Hancock's Half Hour and Round The Horne.

KENNETH WILLIAMS

THE ACTORS' CHURCH
ST PAUL'S BEDFORD STREET COVENT GARDEN LONDON WC2
THURSDAY 29 SEPTEMBER 1988 AT 12 NOON

HYMN

All things bright and beautiful,
All creatures great and small,
All things wise and wonderful
The Lord God made them all.

Each little flower that opens,
Each little bird that sings,
He made their glowing colours,
He made their tiny wings.

The cold wind in the winter,
The pleasant summer...

REMEMBERING KENNETH

EILEEN ATKINS

KENNETH CONNOR

SHEILA HANCOCK

GORDON JACKSON

DEREK NIMMO

LANCE PERCIVAL

NED SHERRIN

BARBARA WINDSOR

Stars raise the roof for tragic Carry On Ken

By ROGER TAVENER, Showbusiness Reporter

THEY carried on laughing as Kenneth Williams' memorial service yesterday—just as Britain's best loved...

Memorial services

Lord Clanmorris
A service of thanksgiving for the life of Lord Clanmorris (John Bingham) was held yesterday at St George's, Hanover Square. The Ven Derek Hayward officiated.

Mr Royd Barker read the lesson, Mrs Peter Johnston read A Time to Dance by Day Lewis and Miss Sheila Mitchell read from a ninth century lament. Mr Terence Brady, son-in-law, gave an address. Among those present were:

Mr Kenneth Williams
A service of thanksgiving for the life of Mr Kenneth Williams was held yesterday at the Actors' Church, St Paul's, Covent Garden. The Rev Michael Hurst-Bannister, Senior Chaplain of the Actors' Church Union, officiated.

Miss Eileen Atkins read from The Waste Land by T.S. Eliot and Miss Sheila Hancock read from The Boy Actor by Noel Coward. Mr Kenneth Connor, accompanied by Mr Gordon Jackson (piano), sang from Kenneth Williams's songs and Miss Barbara Windsor, accompanied by Mr Richard Holmes (piano), sang The Boy I Love. Mr Derek Nimmo, Mr Lance Percival and Mr Ned Sherrin gave addresses. Others present included:

Kenneth Charles Williams
22 February 1926 – 15 April 1988

Kenneth, My Godfather

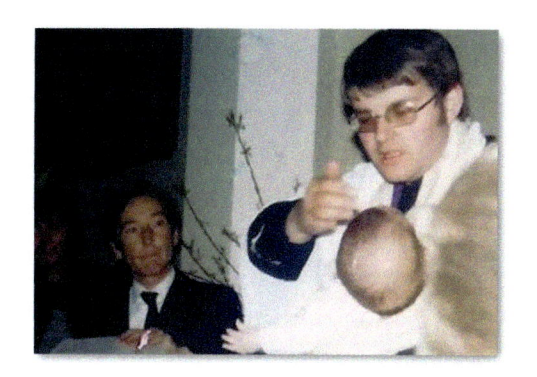

Kenneth became friends with my Grandma's brother John Vere, way back in the 1940's I believe. A long time ago way before he was famous. My Dad said he remembers going out for a family meal where Kenneth had been invited and my Dad being a self conscious ten year old boy was extremely embarrassed as Kenneth was in full flow, getting the attention of the whole restaurant just by being his outrageous self - but that was Kenneth, he could switch it on and engage people. Whether it was a one to one or an audience with, he was brilliant at engaging everyone and then dazzling them with his wit, humour, intelligence and quickness, he was one of a kind.

We miss him because he was just that, one of a kind, and people like that are hard to come by, with his over the top gasps about whatever it may be on his many tv appearances, his razor sharp wit, and his unique sounding voice, which would cut the air the second he spoke. Kenneth was an unusual human being, with an ability seldom seen. One of the things I really liked about Kenneth was how he would say what he thought, he would sometimes start arguments on interviews in a heated debate, he had strong points of view, and unlike so many agreeable people he would speak up! A rare quality I always look for in humans.

I only met Kenneth once when I was ten, though I very much wish I could have met him more. He did carry me at my Christening, which I cannot remember, but my father can, saying how funny it was. Kenneth was taking the Christening very seriously, having to repeat after the vicar as he was sworn in as my Godfather, but with the sound of his theatrical voice ringing round this church in Highgate in North London as if it were a play, piercing the air in his unmistakable way.

When I did meet Kenneth at my Grandma's flat in 1985, I remember him making me laugh until my stomach hurt, he was switched on and in good humour, and would also send me birthday cards and keep in touch with me and my family - we were lucky to have had a connection with him. I also remember when he died, I was twelve, and my Mum told me on the way home from school, and that I had been included in his will, to this day I still do not know why, but I am eternally grateful to him.

Part of the legalities included that I could go to his flat in the Centre of London and just take things, personal possessions of his for me to keep, which I found very strange, and when my Mum and I went into his flat I was instantly struck by how plain it was. This larger than life character just lived in the simplest of flats, which emphasised that there was the showbiz side of Kenneth, and the quiet private side. I also have a few of his smaller week by week diary's at home, and I have looked through them many times, they read Monday - shopping, Tuesday - dentist, then SHOW, SHOW. When I read this it re-affirmed the two opposing sides to his life, which all famous people must experience to varying degrees. I thought how it must have got tiring for him to have to keep switching on the Kenneth we have seen on the telly so much, and then reverting to his normal self in private, maybe I am wrong but I imagine it was tiring.

I miss him greatly, we all do, and I believe we can all carry on Kenneth's spirit in our daily lives by being a bit more daring, a bit wilder, pushing the boundaries a little more, asking a few more questions, and saying what we think. Anyway all our love goes out to you Kenneth, thank you for being you, we will never forget you and 'stop messing about!'

Robert Chidell, 2018

Kenneth, My Friend

I started off as a fan but was lucky enough for Kenneth to want me as a friend, which matured considerably over the fifteen years until his death. Between meetings we kept in touch by letters as he knew I liked receiving letters and he enjoyed writing them, trying out different pen styles. I have 120 letters, varying in size from one page A5 to four pages A4.

I wrote to Kenneth in February 1973 asking to meet him after his performance in the play *My Fat Friend*. He replied saying he could not meet, due to filming. Determined to meet him, I went down to London anyway and my first meeting with Kenneth was on 4 April 1973, outside The Globe Theatre after seeing him in the play. When he found out I was from Hull, he made the assumption, as many others did, that I worked with fish, asking "Did I work in the gutting sheds?" I retorted, "I've never even seen one, let alone been in one." He replied, "You live in Hull and have never seen a gutting shed?" I snapped back, "We're not just a fishing village, you know!" He then said, "If you're down this way again, drop a note in at the theatre and come around for drinks." Barbara Windsor, years later said to me, that is why Kenneth liked you, because you snapped back at him! Two days later, I attended a recording of the radio show, *More Secret Life of Kenneth Williams*. They didn't need a warm-up person because Kenneth came out and did the job himself!

My first visit to a *Just A Minute* recording was in 1974 through to my last in 1988. Kenneth would always arrange the tickets for us, which were reserved. We would always sit with Louie and afterwards would go for either a drink or, more usually, a meal. He would always come out last to great applause. You could always tell what sort of mood he was in, whether we had to rush out before people wanted an autograph, or he would ask "Does anyone want an autograph?" After one *Just A Minute* recording, he took us for a drink. My husband, Tony, took some photos of us both and Kenneth said "Let's give them something to talk about" by giving me a kiss!

In November 1975, he sent me a very long typed letter, which reads like a Carry On script, giving a description of his hand operation and falling about laughing continuously from being given too much nitrous oxide anaesthetic (What film does this remind you of?) Tony and I had just got engaged and Kenneth was staggered when I told him. He had to have a fag and a glass of Andrews (fizzy health drink) and re-read my letter!

When introducing us to people we did not know, he would always say, "These are my friends Barbara and Tony, from Hull in East Yorkshire. I have to say East Yorkshire otherwise she goes absolutely wild if I put Humberside on her letters. They call them Waslin-Ashbridge, because she wouldn't give her name up when they got married. Queen Victoria gave hers up changing it from Saxe-Coburg-Saalfeld to Saxe-Coburg and Gotha, but not Barbara." He then had the cheek to use it when standing in as presenter of *Wogan* on 25 April 1986. When I wrote to him saying about it, he said, "Well it sounds so POSH and ACADEMIC!"

On one occasion, he sent me a cassette tape called *Parlour Poetry* that he had just recorded, commenting that it had been an interesting challenge and fascinating to think how this stuff held our forefathers entranced.

He would always send me his books and the publicity cards etc. The *Acid Drops* postcard talks about what would be the *Chaos Supersedes ENSA* programme for Southern TV and mentions about directing *Loot*, which we went to see. He said as the director he had to be very strict but discovered that there was more to directing than he first thought. On the card he calls me a 'loyal soul' and would often refer to me as his 'loyal old chum' (one that never lets you down). As a special favour to me, he signed the *Back Drops* book as 'Kenneth Charles Williams'. *Just Williams* was due to be called *Scene Drops*, and then it changed to *Exception of the Day*, before becoming *Just Williams*.

When he was on the radio programme, *Bookshelf* in December 1980 reviewing the Henry VIII book, I wrote saying, how good it sounded and it arrived in the post the next day along with a letter. He later commented to me, that he had found the book turgid and I was a better man than he, to be able to read it!

In many of his letters he would go into some detail about his many medical problems and always valued my opinion. I do not think he was a hypochondriac, but was just sensitive about his health.

One very nice letter was when he was making the programme *Comic Roots* in August 1983. He enclosed a photograph, saying that there should have been a bubble coming out of his mouth saying "What was that song I was going to sing for Barbara."

His very last words to me were – "you should not make arrangements with tottering old men!" (as he had to cancel our meet-up in April 1988, due to being in so much pain).

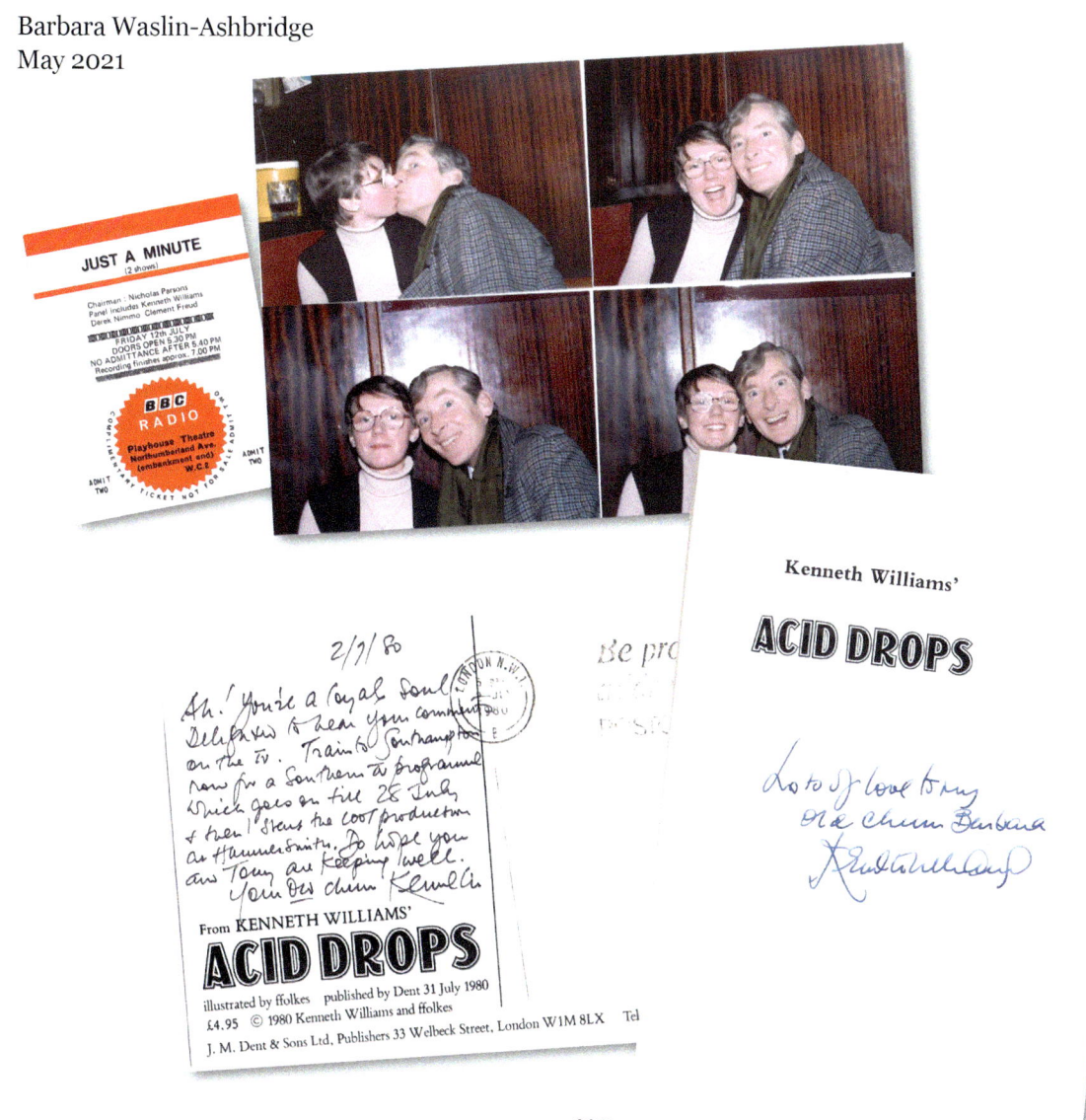

Barbara Waslin-Ashbridge
May 2021

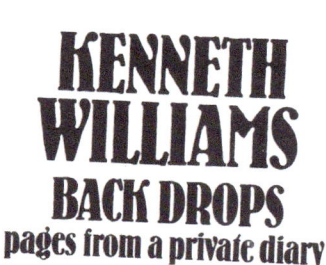

KENNETH WILLIAMS
BACK DROPS
pages from a private diary

DRAWINGS BY LARRY

lots of love Barbara
from (Ken Williams)

J M Dent & Sons Ltd
London Melbourne Toronto

Just Williams
The Autobiography of

KENNETH WILLIAMS

Publication 19th September
£8·95 DENT

FROM KENNETH WILLIAMS   10.12.80.

Dear Barbara
 For your Greetings Card + letter today — many thanks — Off now to Brighton for book signing session — am sending you the Henry song 'cos if you can get thro' this then you're a better man than I am. Love to Tony
 Kenneth

6, MARLBOROUGH HOUSE, OSNABURGH STREET, LONDON, NW1 3LY

31 August '83

Dear Barbara
 there should be a bubble coming out of my mouth saying "What was that song I was going to sing for Barbara?" Shan't aver here? It's a still from Comic Roots which I've done for the BBC. Off now to rehearse Jackanory at TV Centre. Hope you + Tony are keeping well
 Yours
 Kenneth

Meeting Kenneth

"He's very thin, and he talks a lot about wanking."

Such was my introduction to Kenneth Williams by his friend Michael Whittaker, after I'd enquired if there was anything I should know in advance. He also advised me not to ask what Tony Hancock and Joe Orton were like, or to mention the Carry On films.

We went to Joe Allen, the restaurant in Exeter Street favoured by the theatrical profession. We sat in the far corner, close to the kitchen. At 19:45 precisely, as Michael had predicted, Kenneth arrived. "He's here," I said, watching him hand over his grey overcoat to the cloakroom attendant. I recognised him instantly. He walked over and Michael introduced us. We shook hands. I was struck how smartly dressed he was, in a blue suit and crocheted tie. He was indeed thin, and I was slightly intimidated by his hooded eyelids.

He threw me straight away – he was under the impression I was some sort of intellectual (I was actually a trainee teacher) - and asked if I knew the answer to the Telegraph crossword clue he couldn't get. I had no idea.

Michael, ever the diplomat, kept things going and as the wine arrived and the waiter brought the menu, things became more relaxed. Kenneth, who wore his glasses to peruse the menu, said – in a tone of resignation - "Oh, I'll just have the burger." This was Joe Allen's famous, but secret, off-menu beefburger. This was the only point of the evening when he seemed tired to me. When I read the published diary entry for the day before, it made sense: "I'm brimful with depression and suicidal theories. How quickly and easily could one make an END?"

Over the food and wine the conversation became more lively and inhibtions were shed on all sides. I'm afraid I did ask him about the Carry Ons – his favourite was Matron, he said, and when I asked why Emmanuelle had been such a flop he said (with relish) "It has this woman – it was a long dinner table in an embassy – and she was under the table, sucking cocks!" There followed many funny stories and bitchy anecdotes about various showbiz people.

After a most enjoyable dinner, the three of us walked from Exeter Street to the Strand where Michael had parked his Jaguar. I felt totally elated walking alongside him (he'd put on the cap he used to avoid recognition, but there were still several doubletakes from passers-by). It was an extraordinary feeling. Although Kenneth had walked to Joe's, Michael was giving him a lift back to Osnaburgh Street. I got into the passenger seat, and Kenneth sat in the back. As we drove towards Embankment Tube station (I was staying with a friend in New Cross) Kenneth said how nice my hair looked. I had to admit I'd dyed it. Earlier in the evening – discussing my letters in which I'd admitted a lack of confidence when it came to dating – he said he was surprised and said I was "a dish" - with a very Celtic face.

As we pulled in near the station, I thanked Michael profusely. Kenneth got out of the back of the car and pointed me in the right direction to the underground. Just before he returned to the passenger seat, I wished him goodnight. "Bye bye, my love, " he said.

Eight weeks later, he was gone.

Nick Lewis
May 2021

Afterword by Robin Sebastian

I first saw Kenneth Williams in *Carry on Cowboy* on TV in the early 1970's and I was hooked! At boarding school, we had music appreciation lessons and a treat for us was to play a song at the end of each class by Rambling Syd Rumpo from T*he Best of Rambling Syd Rumpo*, recorded in front of a particularly lively, and as it turned out, well oiled audience at Abbey Road Studio. My favourite was *What Shall We Do With the Drunken Nurker?* which simply had us all in stitches! I subsequently bought the album in the holiday and played it incessantly! Obviously I loved mimicking and Kenneth was prime material, as I noticed he could extract humour from nothing!

When I left drama school in 1992, I blossomed into nonentity! The big change in my career was when I became aware of my knack for "doing Kenneth". I was working as a wine waiter in London, like Julian and Sandy filling in between engagements... I was a 'resting actor', so much so that I was practically in a coma! I was wandering round topping the guests up with fizz exclaiming remarks like "Do you fancy another bottle up your end?" etc. all a la Mr Williams. When one of the guests, the talented actor Nigel Lindsay approached me and said "you do Kenneth Williams?" To which I replied "well, yes". He told me he was just finishing at the National in *The London Cuckolds* directed by Terry Johnson, who was desperately trying to find a Kenneth for his forthcoming production of *Cleo, Camping, Emmanuelle and Dick* and that I should send him a tape. A week later I received a letter from Terry thanking me for my tape, but the part had already gone to the excellent Adam Godley. It planted the idea in my head that maybe I could play the great man.

It was not until September 2003 that I was asked to audition for a fringe production of *Round The Horne Revisited* at the White Bear in Kennington. The show was the brainchild of Barry Took, who just wanted this wonderful material to be shared with a modern audience. Sadly Barry died before it got off the ground and sometime later Brian Cooke decided to test the water with a compilation of his favourite Horne morsels.

Well the show was an enormous success! I remember our opening night... this tiny theatre was jam-packed! It was standing room only and people had flocked from all over the UK to be at the very spot where this golden material was being recreated... the audience went wild! The critics were full of praise and as a result, we transferred to the Leicester Square Theatre for a run that lasted sixteen months, with a BBC TV special.

Each night, certainly in the first six months of the run, we were sold out and were inundated by so many celebrities who came to see our show, many of whom would stay for a glass of champagne after. We had Sir Tim Rice, Lord Andrew Lloyd Webber, Amanda Barrie, Barry Cryer, June Whitfield, Lorraine Chase, Nicholas Parsons etc. Best of all for me was having a drink with the punters who had loved the show and to hear their experiences of either listening or in many cases knowing Kenneth.

I was next asked to play Kenneth in a new revival called *Round The Horne: Unseen and Uncut*. Lyn Took, Barry's ex-wife, was aiming for authenticity using only Barry and Marty's scripts and accurately recreating the original studio on stage, she also insisted on having the musical interlude reinstated. This was a stroke of genius. We started as a try-out at the Theatre Royal Brighton and it went down very well. We used dummy microphones on stage and had radio microphones hidden in our ties so we were not constrained. As a result of the success of the week, we embarked on a tour the following year. Brian Cooke then bounced back with the sequel to *Round the Horne* entitled *Stop Messing About*, which had come about on the radio when Kenneth Horne died in 1969. In the stage version, Brian had decided to make it a variety show comprising material he had also written for other people. The characters of Julian and Sandy remained but due to a fear of being sued, Brian made them a brother and sister team from Birmingham, interviewed by me as the Horne type character. The confusion from the audiences was evident. We opened for a five-week run at the Leicester Square theatre. Even though the reviews for *Stop Messing About* were disappointing about the material, we proceeded on a six month tour.

While that was being planned, Jonathan Rigby and I were approached to play our respective Kenneths by Wes Butters in a one-off radio show called *Twice Ken is Plenty*. Wes had obtained this previously unperformed script and had been written by Horne and Mollie Millest. Incidentally, she had become a writer for Horne and Richard Murdoch as a teenager. The script was incomplete, but Jonathan and I got together and filled in the missing links. The story centred around the two Kenneths making their way through the various departments of the BBC, playing all the different characters who worked there. I am delighted to say, it went down a storm with the audience at the BBC Radio Theatre and was aired on Radio 4!

The next chapter in my 'Kenneth' career began when Neil Pearson contacted me to ask if I would like to play Williams in a series of lost recordings of *Hancock's Half Hour* on Radio 4. I thought... Ooh, how thrilling! I said a big yes! He then found the brilliant Kevin McNally to play Hancock and the show was an instant success. Having recorded two series of the *Missing Hancocks*, the new commissioner of the BBC Radio 4 decided not to do anymore, despite the show's phenomenal success along with CD sales. After an outcry on social media however, the BBC came back saying that we had misunderstood their intentions and that we would be commissioned again. Nevertheless, in 2006 I travelled to Glasgow to film *Hancock's Half Hour* for BBC 4 in front of a live studio audience, always preferable to a dead one! I was so nervous as I had never done a sitcom in front of an audience before! I had no need to panic as Kevin McNally made mistake after mistake after mistake and won the audience over with his hilarious adlibs! The show was great success for BBC4 and lots of fun to perform!

In 2016, I landed the role of Kenneth in the biographical film Babs, showcasing the live of Barbara Windsor. I had three small scenes and one of them was a recreation of *Carry On Spying!* I thought this thrilling! We filmed it at Hither Green Studios in South London and it took ages! Continuity was very tricky, trying to remember which hand my cloak was in and which the hat! We were shooting it from seven different angles - at least I can say I was sort of in a Carry On film!

Brian Cooke reformed most of the *Round The Horne...Revisited* cast in 2018 to perform *Stop Messin' About* material reformatted to the Horne team under the title of Horne Aplenty and we performed it back at the White Bear. It went down very well indeed.

To sum up, if it was not for Kenneth Williams and his legacy, I do not know whether I would still be an actor! His sheer brilliance and ability to amuse and make people laugh, has allowed me to recreate that magic and give audiences the opportunity to enjoy the overwhelming warmth, wit and nostalgia of the great man himself!

Robin Sebastian, May 2021

Afterword by Bill Holland

Kenneth Williams is, indisputably, a universal character. He thought himself merely a cult figure, yet he rests in the mind's eye of every Briton worthy of the name. Kenneth remains fresh and vibrant and more than three decades after his demise, part of us.

He is certainly part of me. I travelled the typical enthusiasts' path from casual admirer to avid fan, and thence to ardent devotee. I caught the bug, however, *after* his death, during the period that his posthumous reputation was being formed. Kenneth's oeuvre was there to be enjoyed - and enjoy it I did - but the man himself, now out of the way, was up for evaluation. This spell of analysis came to a head in 1993 with the publishing of his infamous personal diaries, the surviving forty-three volumes of which were carefully edited and condensed into an 800-page bestseller. Whilst many notable journals are illuminating in their own specific way (Samuel Pepys' as a first-hand chronicle of Restoration London, Captain Scott's for its steadfast heroism, Virginia Woolf's in her approach to artistic origination), Kenneth's is the whole kit and caboodle. From initial scenes of wartime life for a petulant, misplaced Cockney stripling, right through to the dispiriting final days of the lonely, ailing celebrity, each entry is a fervent, belletristic grenade. Chock-full of waggish mudslinging, astringent self-criticism, ribald starry narrative, scurrilous gay gossip, maddening hypochondriacal wittering, profound intellectual contemplation and simple, laugh-out-loud recollection, the Williams diary plots a bewildering chart, flitting from childlike delight to crippling despair, from crude exhibitionism to puritanical repression.

Watching Kenneth bring grinning havoc to a scene in *Hancock's Half Hour*, or hearing him pertly spout Polari-infused repartee in a Julian and Sandy skit, it is hard to envisage a blither spirit. Indeed, some of the disclosed account reinforces this notion of an uproarious personality - a camp, capricious clown, fully aligned with his public roles. What surprised me though, and has fascinated me ever since I first picked up a copy of the book, is how much of it contradicts this image altogether. For example, one can listen to a virtuoso performance from a recording of *Just a Minute*, where Kenneth's exorbitant, gut-busting display has a helpless audience eating out of the palm of his hand… and then turn to the corresponding page of the diary and discover that he loathed every second of it, detested his co-stars, felt deep guilt for his grandstanding behaviour, and could not wait to return to his chaste, spartan flat to purge his sins, with mournful, Teutonic lieder as the accompanying soundtrack. You can see why I was hooked!

Kenneth's journal is far more than simply a record of events. Though he indicated that it was begun when he was fourteen in order to monitor his progress as a trainee draughtsman, the diary quickly became an ersatz partner. He wrote down what he thought and felt, because - behind closed doors - there was nobody else to tell. Despite this state of solitude being a vehement choice, his cogitations still needed to be expelled and registered. True, his glorious mother Louie, was only next door and he had a cluster of chums close at hand - but that just did not cut the mustard: it all needed setting out, neatly, via a fountain pen.

The Kenneth Williams Diaries quickly became my favourite book, my go-to in any number of situations. Whether buoyant or in a melancholy mood, I could always find a felicitous passage. If a famous event or personage from yesteryear was brought up in conversation, out came my battered paperback for an index-skim to see if Kenneth had had an opinion.

He invariably had.

Being such a weighty tome, it is surprising that the printed edition of the diary represents only twenty percent of the several million words that he set to paper between 1942 and 1988. Whilst I thought it inconceivable that the original manuscripts could possibly contain dull or easily expungable sections, it was not a stretch to imagine that some cuts had been unavoidable, thanks to the 'brazen' nature of the content. Keen to see for myself, I contacted an apropos assistant at the British Library, which has been the archive's home since its acquisition in 2015. Despite never having visited this institution, I knew it was no common-or-garden lending library. I presumed that, as a layman, I would receive the polite brush-off, and that ultimately I had about as much chance of getting up close and personal with the Kenneth Williams collection as I had of nipping to the Tower to try the Imperial State Crown for size. To my surprise and delight, the curator seemed happy to hear from me and pleased to help.

The anticipation of viewing valuable articles is only enhanced by the formalities that accompany the process. After proving my identity, announcing the purpose of my visit and agreeing to adhere to the rules, I waited at the Reading Room counter as the assistant went round the back to fetch my quarry. It was like standing in the world's poshest, quietest branch of Argos. The excitement rose with my heart rate in the knowledge that I was to be allowed to peruse the great man's confidential daybooks, essentially unsupervised, for as long as I wished.

One person's Dead Sea Scrolls are another person's scrap paper, so I know these things are relative. But being able to touch items that Kenneth Williams used and, in many ways, relied upon in his most eremitic moments, and to study the private ponderings within, is acutely special. Subject matter aside, the most striking element of the diaries is the *beauty* and variety of Kenneth's penmanship. His calligraphic style, and even the size of the script and the colour of the ink he chooses, festoons and augments the text, as do the photos and clippings which are abundantly dispersed throughout. Very few things please me more than a brand new book - the crisp leaves, the sharply aligned edges and radiant monochrome typeface... but like a Barbaresco, a stilton or a joke, the old ones are always the best. The smoky vanilla scent of the autumnally yellowing pages, the thumb-made scratches and dints of repeated handling, the soft and dusty sweep of parched sheets: Kenneth's diary is spry and humming, in both a literary and sensory sense.

The diaries might be alive and well but, alas, the great man is not. Leaving us at the age of 62 with the oft-repeated "Oh - what's the bloody point?" as his final, bitter poser, we are left behind trying to find answers. While others examine the evidence prudently, I have taken the 'what if' proposition to its logical(ish) conclusion. I have started to imagine a continuing, enduring Kenneth Williams, a Kenneth Williams that lived on into the 1990s. I am currently in the process of extending the diary by ten years and using my accumulated knowledge of Kenneth and his journal to invent fictional avenues for him to explore, and put this wonderful, complicated, mercurial, perspicacious, brilliant, *funny* little chap into an alternate Britain of my generation. I know it is terribly bold of me to attempt to capture the essence of this entertainment legend, and I hope I will not appear conceited. But at the end of the day, Kenneth's my hero, one of our country's most loved comedy actors, and I miss him. I want him to carry on.

Bill Holland, June 2021

Acknowledgements

There are many people that I wish to thank for making this *Scrapbook* possible and have shared their treasures and collections with me, in no particular order:

Firstly, my very good friend and guardian of an archive of Kenneth's letters, Stephen Milverton who has kindly shared much of his collection with me, including a wealth of letters from the Pat Williams Estate.

Morris Bright MBE for his generous support and allowing the use of images from the collection of Peter Rogers via a letter from Peter received in 2006. Great illustrations from the *Carry On* series and others.

Barbara and Tony Waslin-Ashbridge for their friendship, immense support and contribution.

Robert Chidell for his encouragement and allowing me to reproduce his words written for the book launch of *The Kenneth Williams Companion* in April 2018.

Nick Lewis for being a great chum and sharing his memories and collection.

Robin Sebastian for taking the time to write an afterword and for his absolute generosity and support.

Bill Holland and his father Keith for assisting in the research of Kenneth's family tree and writing an afterword – Bill's book is the next to look forward to!

Peter Cadley for his immense kindness in sharing the private collection from the Estate of Rt. Hon George Borwick.

Vincenzo (Enzo) Catapano for the super photos of Michael Anderson and his support.

Beverlie Manson for being so kind with her time and sharing the photos of her and Kenneth at the book signing of *I Only Have to Close My Eyes*.

Bobbie Spargo and Andrew Merriman, both for their generosity and support in sharing images from their father's collections, Nicholas Spargo and Eric Merriman respectively.

Sacha Mendy for her time in recalling the Morgan family tree and sharing some photos from the family archive.

David Benedictius for his stills from *Catch As Catch Can* and the late Adrian Brown for allowing me access to the archive for his production of *The Noble Spaniard*, he was a great advocate for my work.

Baroness Floella Benjamin DBE for the image from *Signed and Sealed*.

Stanley Baxter for all his support and use of images from his private archive.

Anthony Howarth for the reproduction of images he took of Kenneth in 1967.

Barney Bowe for the lovely photo with Kenneth on the set of the Dylon commercial.

Matthew E. Banks for allowing the use of photos from Newquay period of Kenneth's life and his support.

Fellow author and friend Sebastian Lassandro for images of *Cinderella*.

The late Peter Nichols for granting permission to reproduce from his book.

Christopher Naylor for his absolutely amazing caricature drawing of Kenneth that he drew especially for this book.

Fellow fans, Sam Bessant, Gillian Bryant, Paul Howe, Kevin McEwen, Eddie Moss, Steve O'Brien, Paul Simpson and Chris Winwood.

With thanks also to the Estate of Kenneth Williams, John Buss, Archivist at Devonshire Park Theatre, The Blake Museum in Bridgwater and the female on a Facebook group who allowed permission to use images of Kenneth taken by her grandfather during his time in the army.

Also, not forgetting the support of my family and friends for this project, including fellow Fantom author, Kevin Geddes.

List of Illustrations

Every effort has been made to trace copyright holders, but any who have been overlooked are invited to get in touch with the publishers.

All photographs, programmes, posters, leaflets, covers and other memorabilia not specifically credited are from the author's own collection.

Cover: Newquay portrait, courtesy of Matthew E Banks; Willo the Wisp, courtesy of Bobbi Spargo, used with permission; *Carry On Cleo* and *Carry On Behind* stills, Peter Rogers, courtesy of Morris Bright MBE; Holiday snap, The Estate of Rt. Hon George Borwick, copyright to Peter Cadley

iii, illustrations from *Kenneth Williams: In His Own Words* (Double Yellow TV/Channel 5) by Charles Waples, used with permission; iv, Michael Anderson, courtesy of Vincenzo Catapano; viii & ix, images supplied by Morris Bright MBE; xi, original letter from the collection of Stephen Milverton; xiii, Pat Williams wedding, courtesy of Imperial War Museum

The Scrapbook: 1, *The Rose and the Ring*, The Estate of Kenneth Williams; 3, reproduced by permission of the late Peter Nichols; 5-7, from the collection of Matthew E Banks; 9, theatre bills supplied by John Buss, Archivist, Devonshire Park Theatre; 11, stills supplied by The Blake Museum, Bridgwater, *The Beggar's Opera*, Rex Features; 15, original letter from the collection of Stephen Milverton; 26, Kenneth and Pat, used with permission from Sacha Mendy; 27, courtesy of the late Adrian Brown, used with permission; 28-29, various from The Estate of Rt. Hon George Borwick, copyright to Peter Cadley; 34-36, original letters from the collection of Stephen Milverton; 41, stills courtesy of David Benedictus, used with permission and original letter from the collection of Stephen Milverton; 43, Kenneth and Joan on set, Rex Features; 44, tickets from the collections of Paul Howe and Stephen Milverton, Kenneth with John Law, Anthony Howarth, used with permission; 47, *Frost On Sunday* images, Rex Features; 48, Kenneth and Frankie Howerd, Rex Features, Kenneth in his flat, Anthony Howarth, used with permission; 49, Kenneth laughing, Anthony Howarth, used with permission; 50-52, original letters from the collection of Stephen Milverton; 54-55, photos courtesy of Stanley Baxter, Vincenzo Catapano and The Estate of Rt. Hon George Borwick, copyright to Peter Cadley; 59-60, original letters from the collection of Stephen Milverton; 64, Kenneth and Lou, used with permission from Sacha Mendy, original letter from the collection of Stephen Milverton; 69, *Russell Harty Plus*, Rex Features; 72, pages from original script from the collection of Stephen Milverton; 73, original letter from the collection of Stephen Milverton, cartoon image supplied by Nigel Rees, used with permission; 77, photo supplied by Baroness Floella Benjamin DBE; 79, *Night of 100 Stars*, Rex Features; 80, portrait, Rex Features; 84, with June Whitfield and Kenneth Connor, Rex Features; 86, Hattie Jacques Memorial Service, Rex Features; 87, *Whizzkids Guide* portrait, Rex Features; 88, courtesy of Bobbi Spargo, used with permission; 91, original letter from the collection of Stephen Milverton; 92, Kenneth with glass, Rex Features; 92-93, original letters from the collection of Stephen Milverton; 94, main *Countdown* photo, Rex Features; 96-99, *An Audience With* images, Rex Features; 100, signing at the stage door, Eddie Moss, Dylon advert, photo supplied by Barney Bowe, used with permission; 101, *Carry On Laughing's Christmas Classics*, Rex Features; 102, main *Some You Win* images, Rex Features; 105, main portrait, Rex Features; 106, with Lou, Michael Whittaker, used with permission, clutching book, Rex Features, book signing, Paul Simpson, used with permission; 107, book signing, Beverlie Manson, used with permission; 107-108, original letters from the collection of Stephen Milverton; 108-109, original letters from the collection of Steve O'Brien; 109, main portrait, Rex Features; 115, Robert Chidell, used with permission, 117-118, from the collection of Barbara Waslin-Ashbridge, used with permission; 119, Nick Lewis, used with permission; 120-121, Robin Sebastian, used with permission; 122, Bill Holland, used with permission.

All *Carry On* images, Peter Rogers, courtesy of Morris Bright MBE

Adam Endacott

Adam Endacott is a Kenneth Williams aficionado and dedicated fan since early childhood. He has spent his life documenting and collecting everything Kenneth!
A Creative & Communications Director who lives in London, this is his third book. Adam has also worked as a consultant on several Kenneth documentaries. He is pictured here with Lorraine Chase at the book launch of *The Kenneth Williams Companion*.